MW00759921

SRA
Reading
Mastery®
Transformations

Reading
Textbook B

Siegfried Engelmann

Owen Engelmann

Karen Davis

Mc
Graw
Hill

Acknowledgments

The authors are grateful to the following people for their assistance in the preparations of Reading Mastery Transformations Grade 1 Reading.

Joanna Jachowicz
Blake Engelmann
Charlene Tolles-Engelmann
Cally Dwyer
Melissa Morrow
Toni Reeves

Emily Jachowicz for her valuable student input

We'd also like to acknowledge, from McGraw Hill, the valuable contributions by:

Mary Eisele
Nancy Stigers
Jason Yanok

mheducation.com/prek-12

Copyright © 2021 McGraw-Hill Education

All rights reserved. No part of this publication may be reproduced or distributed in any form or by any means, or stored in a database or retrieval system, without the prior written consent of McGraw-Hill Education, including, but not limited to, network storage or transmission, or broadcast for distance learning.

Send all inquiries to:
McGraw-Hill Education
8787 Orion Place
Columbus, OH 43240

ISBN: 978-0-07-905404-3
MHID: 0-07-905404-8

Printed in the United States of America.

2 3 4 5 6 7 8 9 LWI 24 23 22 21

1. hol_e_s
2. taking
3. compl_a_n
4. tripped
5. hanging
6. orders

1. wa_tch_
2. wa_sh
3. give
4. should
5. looked
6. would

1. roar_ed_
2. starts_
3. plans_
4. blam_ed_
5. sav_ing_
6. bit_e_r

1. t_r_ail
2. joking
3. hik_e_r
4. lin_e_d
5. go_e_s
6. making

The Little Bug Bites
Part Two

Jill's brother was stuck in a spider web. The spider was creeping closer and closer to Jill's brother. He was scared. So were the others. "What can we do?" Jill asked.

The little bug said, "We can do some big time biting." The little bug jumped down into the web and started to bite a hole in the web. Then he told Jill's brother, "Jump down into this hole, and you will be safe."

But the spider was now very close, and it looked very mean. The little bug looked at the spider and said, "Stay back, or I will take a big bite out of you."

The spider smiled and said, "You make me laugh. Show me your best bite."

The little bug showed his teeth and said, "This is how my bite starts out. Then I open wide and roar like this." The bug opened up so wide and made such a big roar that it almost sent the spider flying.

3

The spider ran and hid while the little bug and Jill's brother got out of the web.

After the bugs were safe, Jill gave the little bug a big hug. Then she told him, "You are such a good biter. Thank you for saving my brother."

The end.

baby

1. On line 1, tell who will walk.

2. On line 2, tell who will sleep.

A man grabbed two stones at the beach and took them home. Those stones were really turtles. When the man got home, he set the turtles in his back yard.

When he came back, he said, "My stones are walking back to the beach."

The man helped the turtles back to the beach.

1. What did the man think he grabbed at the beach?
2. What did the man really grab?
3. Where did the man set them?
4. Where did the turtles go?

62

1. load
2. second
3. kept
4. sneeze
5. slide
6. racket

1. watched
2. girls
3. blamed
4. riding
5. dirty
6. painted

1. taking
2. making
3. joking
4. waking
5. talking
6. telling
7. cleaning

1. bat
2. bar
3. duck
4. tool
5. skin
6. glid

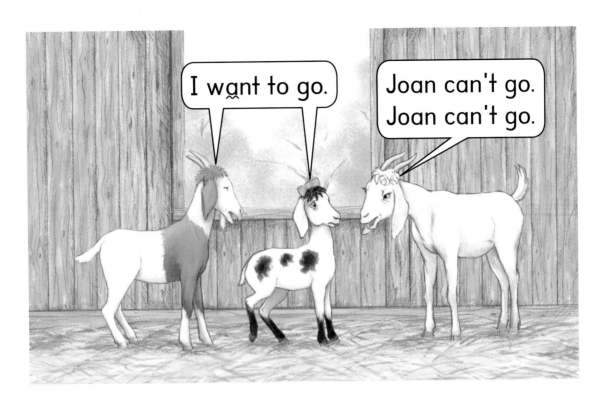

The Big Goat Hike
Part One

Nine goats made plans to go on a hike. They were going to follow a trail over five hills.

Joan was one of the goats who planned to go on this hike. Gorman also planned to go. But Joan's mom did not like that part of the plan.

She did not want Joan to get wet or to get dirty. She blamed Gorman for what happened the last time Joan went with him. So she told the other goats, "If Gorman goes, Joan stays home. If Gorman goes, Joan stays home."

Joan did not want to stay home. She kept telling her mom that she would not walk near Gorman. She said that no goats would go near the pond because the trail they were taking did not go by any water. She told her mom, "We will be in the hills. We will be in the hills."

But her mom kept telling Joan, "No, you can't go. No, you can't go."

For days, Joan and her mother talked and talked. The more they talked, the more the other goats made jokes about Gorman and the toads.

More to come.

girl

1. On line 1, tell who will skate.
2. On line 2, tell who will eat.

Ann's mom told Ann and her pals to paint the dock green. So the girls got a pail of paint and began to paint. Ann's brother was out boating. So he didn't have to help paint. But Ann's brother got green feet when he got out of the boat and walked on the dock.

1. Who painted the dock?
2. They painted the dock so it was ____.
3. Did Ann's brother help to paint?
4. Her brother got ____ feet.

63

1. plac e
2. pretty
3. would
4. should
5. could

1. washed
2. hiker
3. everybody
4. nobody
5. making
6. listening

1. write
2. steep
3. strike
4. lead
5. led
6. until

1. joking
2. dirty
3. funny
4. skin
5. asking
6. lined

1. trap
2. net
3. wail
4. horse
5. chore
6. third

The Big Goat Hike
Part Two

Joan and her mom talked and talked about the hike in the hills. While they talked, the other goats kept making jokes about Gorman. One goat kept asking, "Gorman, if you go on this hike, should I take my swim things with me?"

Another goat kept saying, "If I go on this hike, will I end up with a toad on my head?"

Oh, how the goats laughed and laughed at these jokes. But Gorman did not think they were very funny.

On the day before the hike, the goats were in the barn making jokes about Gorman and the toads. They stopped joking when they saw Joan and her mother walking over to the barn.

Joan's mother looked very mad. She told the goats, "Joan really wants to go. Joan really wants to go." She told the goats that Joan could not get dirty. Then she told Gorman, "If Joan gets dirty, I will blame you. If Joan gets dirty, I will blame you."

Gorman said, "Well, I . . . I don't know what to say . . . I . . ." Joan and her mother and the goats talked and talked. At last, everybody agreed. Joan would go on the hike, and Gorman would go, too. Nobody would go near water or mud. And Gorman would never lead the way.

More next time.

grass   white   hay

1. On line 1, tell what the black cow eats.

2. On line 2, tell about the other cow.

Three girls said, "Let's go fishing." So they went on a little train to the lake. Then they walked to the fishing hole. They did not come home with any fish because the girls forgot to bring their fishing gear with them. But the girls did jump in the water and took a swim.

1. Who went fishing?

2. What did they ride on?

3. Did they get lots of fish?

4. They forgot to bring their   .

14

64

1. bottom
2. until
3. Ted
4. past
5. sneez**e**
6. led

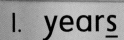

1. year<u>s</u>
2. watch<u>ed</u>
3. inch<u>es</u>
4. bump<u>ed</u>
5. gather<u>ing</u>
6. lik**e**<u>ly</u>

1. off
2. lazy
3. heavy
4. w<u>o</u>rk
5. pla<u>c</u>e
6. <u>or</u>der

1. <u>a</u><u>i</u>r
2. f<u>a</u><u>i</u>r
3. ch<u>a</u><u>i</u>r
4. tool
5. pool
6. out
7. shout

Some animals have prehensile tails.

The Big Goat Hike
Part Three

The goats were ready for the hike. Joan could go with them, but the goats could not go near water or mud. And Gorman would never lead. He would have to stay at the end of the line.

The nine goats lined up. The first goat was named Ted. He was a good hill hiker. So he was the leader. Gorman was the last goat in line. Joan was just in front of him.

The goats followed the trail over three hills. Then they came to a hive of mean bees. Ted said, "We can't go on this trail. We'll have to take the old trail that is next to the lake."

So Ted led the way to the old trail. This trail was very steep, and it went up and up, next to the lake.

When the goats were almost to the top of the hill, they came to a place where the trail stopped. The trail was washed out. Ted told the other goats, "We'll have to go back."

So each goat slowly turned to go back down the trail. Now Ted was not the leader. Ted was at the back end of the line. Who was the leader now? Gorman, that's who.

More to come.

short   eggs

1. On line 1, tell what the long snake eats.
2. On line 2, tell about the other snake.

Last summer, Pam bragged to her pals, "I will swim with otters." They said, "You won't be able to do that." But Pam did swim with otters and other sea mammals. She told everybody how much fun it was to swim with otters and seals. Now, Pam's pals are sick of listening to her.

1. Name two sea mammals Pam swam with.
2. Who did she tell about it?
3. How do her pals feel about listening to Pam now?

65

1. bath
2. pass
3. bump
4. past
5. fourth
6. hooves

1. stories
2. lazy
3. shouted
4. cleaning
5. sliding
6. gliding

1. foot
2. couldn't
3. washing
4. heavy
5. places
6. off

1. driver
2. pancakes
3. hungry
4. complain
5. floated

The Big Goat Hike
Part Four

Way up the old trail, the goats had to turn back because it was washed out. After all of the goats turned, Gorman was the first goat in line.

Joan said, "But Gorman can't lead. But Gorman can't lead."

The other goats told Joan that she would have to be the leader. She would have to go past Gorman. But there was not much room.

Joan told Gorman, "Stand still, and I will pass you. Stand still, and I will pass you."

She started to pass Gorman, but just then, Gorman had to sneeze. He said, "I think I am going . . . to . . ." And he sneezed so hard that he bumped Joan.

She started to slide. So she grabbed on to Gorman and said, "Help, I am slipping. Help, I am slipping."

Both Joan and Gorman slid from the path
all the way to the bottom of the hill. There was
deep mud at the bottom of the hill. Joan and
Gorman slid into that mud and rolled over and
over. When Gorman and Joan stopped, they
looked like mud balls.

The other goats did not want to laugh, but they could not help it. As they watched Gorman and Joan sitting in the mud, they laughed so hard that one of them slid off the path and landed in the mud, too.

This is not the end.

black	cat

1. On line 1, tell what sits on the red car.

2. On line 2, tell about the other car.

Two bugs liked the m<u>oo</u>n. One of them said, "I'm going to fly to the m<u>oo</u>n."

The other bug said, "Me too."

So those bugs started to fly to the m<u>oo</u>n. Then a big balloon floated in front of them.

One bug said, "I do not see the m<u>oo</u>n. I think the m<u>oo</u>n went home."

The other bug said, "Then we sh<u>ou</u>ld go home too." And they did.

1. What did the bugs want to fly to?
2. What went in front of the m<u>oo</u>n?
3. Did the bugs see the m<u>oo</u>n then?
4. Where did the bugs go?

66

1. pretty
2. seconds
3. ch<u>ai</u>rs
4. vehicles
5. stories
6. until

1. look
2. cook
3. couldn't
4. washing
5. heavy
6. write

1. net
2. bath
3. clapped
4. landing
5. strike
6. slid<u>ing</u>

1. serve
2. shape
3. third
4. cry
5. sack
6. drop<u>ed</u>

27

The Big Goat Hike
Part Five

The goats had a good laugh over Joan and Gorman sliding down the hill and landing in a pool of mud. As the goats walked home, the mud on Joan, Gorman, and the other goat started to dry. Soon these goats looked like they were tan dirt cakes.

The other goats laughed and laughed. But when they saw who was waiting at the barn, they stopped laughing. It was Joan's mother.

When Joan saw her mother, she yelled, "Mom, look what happened. Mom, look what happened."

Joan's mother took one look at Joan and said, "Who . . . what? Who . . . what?" Then she looked at the goat next to Gorman and said, "You did this. You did this."

Gorman said, "I had to sneeze. I couldn't help it."

Joan said, "I need a bath. I need a bath."

Her mother said, "Oh, how I hate dirt. Oh, how I hate dirt."

So Joan and her mother left to give Joan a bath. As soon as they were out of the barn, the other goats started to laugh again. But Gorman didn't laugh. He kept saying, "I had to sneeze. I couldn't help it."

After that day, the goats told two stories about Gorman. One was about the time the toads sank his boat. The other was about the time he sneezed on the path.

The end.

black

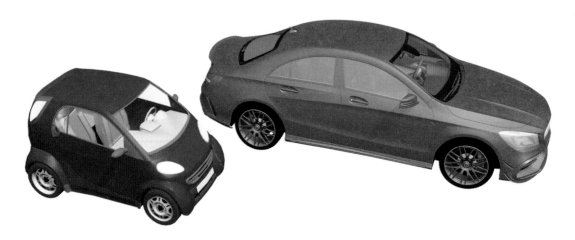

1. On line 1, write what the red car is.

2. On line 2, write about the car that is small.

Debby's tractor didn't run very well. So she took her tractor to Tom's shop. Tom didn't know how to fix the tractor. So Debby traded the tractor for three bikes. She has one big bike and two little ones. She has more fun with her bikes than she did with her tractor.

1. What didn't run very well?

2. Where did Debby take the tractor?

3. Did Tom know how to fix it?

4. She traded her tractor for   .

67

1. foot
2. worker
3. look
4. took
5. watch

1. nod
2. queen
3. buck
4. write
5. fact
6. truck

1. chores
2. roads
3. ships
4. vans
5. rafts

1. reading
2. likely
3. drivers
4. turning
5. hopper
6. wasted
7. glider

1. behind
2. together
3. vehicles
4. balloons
5. airplanes
6. butterfly

Facts about Vehicles

Many vehicles are machines. Cars, trucks, bikes, ships, and many boats, trains, and planes are vehicles that are machines.

Balloons, rafts, hang gliders, and some boats are not machines.

All vehicles take things places. Some vehicles are made to take you and other folks places. Cars, buses, and trains are some of the vehicles that cart folks from place to place.

Other vehicles that take folks and things places go on water. Can you name some of those vehicles?

Yes, row boats, sailboats, rafts, and ships are vehicles that go on water.

Can you name the vehicles that go on rails?

Yes, trains must go on rails to get from place to place. Some trains take folks from place to place. Other trains take things.

Can you name vehicles that go in the air?

Yes, planes, gliders, and hot air balloons go in the air.

Can you name vehicles that go on roads?

Yes, cars, vans, trucks, buses, and bikes go on roads.

Some trucks and trail bikes are made to go places that don't have roads. Off road vehicles go slower but take bumps better than road vehicles.

yellow

1. On line 1, write about the cup that is cold.
2. On line 2, write about the other cup.

A cat was under a ch<u>ai</u>r next to a table. After a while, a man sat to eat at the table. Some food dropped off the table. The cat ate that food.

1. A cat was below a ⬛️.
2. Where was the ch<u>ai</u>r?
3. Who sat to eat?
4. Where did the food the cat ate come from?

68

1. c<u>oo</u>l
2. p<u>oo</u>l
3. c<u>oo</u>k
4. t<u>oo</u>k
5. spri<u>ng</u>
6. bri<u>ng</u>

1. Homer
2. strik<u>e</u>
3. pl<u>ai</u>n
4. f<u>ai</u>r
5. liv<u>es</u>
6. fli<u>es</u>

1. wash<u>ing</u>
2. look<u>ing</u>
3. year<u>s</u>
4. hang<u>ing</u>
5. inch<u>es</u>
6. dropp<u>ing</u>

1. <u>within</u>
2. <u>them</u>selves
3. <u>any</u>thing
4. <u>my</u>self
5. <u>your</u>self
6. <u>it</u>self

The Big Strike
Part One

There were big ants and little ants in an ant hill. For years and years, the big ants gave orders to the little ants. For years and years, the little ants did what the big ants told them to do. If a big ant told little ants to gather seeds, the little ants would gather seeds. If a big ant said, "Drive me to the lake," the little ants would do that. They would get in the ant van and drive the big ant to the lake.

The little ants did all the washing and all the
cleaning and all the other things that had to be
done to keep the ant hill looking good.

As the years went by, the big ants gave more and more orders to the little ants. The little ants started to feel that the big ants were just lazy and mean. But the little ants didn't say anything until one spring day. On that day, a little ant named Homer said, "I just took my last order from those big lazy ants."

A big ant had just ordered the little ants to bring a load of chairs to the swimming pool. "Not me," Homer said. "I'm going on strike."

More next time.

brown	corn

1. On line 1, write what sand is in.

2. On line 2, write about what is in a red bag.

Ann's mom had a van. One day Ann loaded many boots, coats, pants, and shirts inside the van. She also loaded dishes, pots, and pans on the seats. She loaded ch<u>ai</u>rs and a bed on the r<u>oo</u>f. She even loaded a heavy machine in the back of the van. Then she said, "Now there is no room for me in this van."

1. Who had a van?
2. Did Ann load many things into the van?
3. What did Ann load on the r<u>oo</u>f of the van?
4. After Ann loaded the van, there was no room for   .

1. <u>aw</u>ful
2. <u>law</u>n
3. h<u>aw</u>k

1. long
2. song
3. sang
4. hang
5. east
6. l<u>ea</u>st

1. riding
2. glid<u>in</u>g
3. mak<u>in</u>g
4. tak<u>in</u>g
5. t<u>a</u>king
6. walking

1. pretty
2. r<u>oo</u>f
3. quick
4. q<u>u</u>iet
5. within
6. nod

1. racket
2. eye
3. care
4. themselves
5. seconds

The Big Strike
Part Two

Homer had told the other little ants that he was going on strike.

The other little ants asked, "What does that mean, going on strike?"

Homer said, "When you go on strike, you stop doing the things those big ants tell you to do. I think we should all go on strike and let those big ants start taking care of themselves."

The little ants looked at each other, and then some of them said, "Yes, let's go on strike."

Soon the other little ants agreed. "Yes, all of us little ants are going on strike."

One very little ant said, "But now that we are on strike, what will we do?"

Homer said, "Well, we can do anything we want to do."

Somebody asked, "Do you mean we can go swimming?"

"Why not?" Homer said.

Somebody else asked, "Do you mean we can just take the van for a drive?"

"Yes," Homer said. "And I think we should do that now."

Within three seconds, the van was filled with little ants. There were also ants on the roof and ants hanging all over the van. They laughed and sang as Homer drove the van down the road.

More to come.

1. On line 1, write what a cat chases.

2. On line 2, write about a goat.

A girl wanted to make a cake for Mother's Day. The girl asked her older sister to show her how to make a cake. Her sister said, "I'll show you the best way I know to get a cake."

She and her sister gathered their cash. They went to a store and came home with a wonderful cake. It made their mother very happy.

1. Who did the girl ask about making a cake?

2. Where did the girls go?

3. Did they bake a cake or get one at a store?

1. awful
2. hawk
3. yawn
4. lawn
5. draw

1. live
2. live
3. pretty
4. fair
5. care
6. hung

1. scrape
2. shape
3. done
4. won

1. complain
2. ourselves
3. themselves
4. yourself
5. myself

1. dart
2. paths
3. storm
4. mine

1. fields
2. racket
3. watched
4. does

49

The Big Strike
Part Three

The little ants were going for a drive. As Homer drove the van, the other little ants were making an <u>ing</u> an <u>awful</u> racket. They were yelling and singing and telling jokes. At last, Homer drove into a field and stopped.

"What are we going to do here?" some of the ants asked.

Homer said, "I'm going to gather some seeds and eat them myself."

The little ants had never done anything like eating seeds they picked before. At first, they just stood and watched as Homer gathered and ate seeds. Pretty soon, other little ants started doing what Homer was doing. One of the very little ants gathered a big pile of seeds and ate all of them. Then he looked at Homer and said, "Burp."

Just then, ten big ants came up the road. They were not in good shape. They had never walked so far in their lives. Their leader was named Hawk because he looked like a hawk. He said, "You little ants can't strike. It's not fair."

Homer said, "It seems fair to me. We're having a good time."

Hawk said, "The strike is not fair. If you are on strike, who will take care of us?"

Homer said, "You will have to take care of yourself."

One big ant said, "But we don't know how to do that."

More next time.

clean   duck

1. On line 1, write what animal is in a dirty pond.

2. On line 2, write about the other pond.

Dan was eating an ear of corn. A fox tried to trick Dan. The fox told Dan, "Go in back of the tree, and I will show you a funny trick."

Dan left his corn and went in back of the tree. The fox picked up the corn and started to run away with it. The fox tripped and fell into a mole hole. Dan laughed and said, "That is a very funny trick."

1. Who tried to trick somebody?

2. Who did the fox try to trick?

3. What was the fox trying to take from Dan?

4. What did the fox fall in after he tripped?

72

1. l<u>ou</u>d
2. sh<u>ou</u>t
3. h<u>ou</u>se
4. <u>ou</u>r
5. r<u>ou</u>nd

1. s<u>e</u>rve
2. <u>qu</u>it
3. dr<u>aw</u>
4. l<u>aw</u>n

1. <u>compla</u>ning
2. <u>listen</u>ing
3. <u>our</u>selves
4. <u>cry</u>ing
5. <u>gathering</u>

1. room
2. took
3. tired
4. piled
5. been

1. w<u>o</u>rk
2. w<u>ai</u>l
3. hungry
4. rest

The Big Strike
Part Four

The big ants did not want the little ants to strike. The big ants kept saying, "Who will keep the ant hill clean? Who will take us to the p<u>oo</u>l? Who will do all the <u>awful</u> things that must be done?"

Homer said, "I don't know who will do all those things, but we won't, because we are on strike."

Another little ant said, "I feel like going for a swim."

Other ants agreed. So the little ants piled into the ant van and drove to the pool. For a long time, they dove and swam and played water games. This was the first time they had ever been in the pool. Only big ants went in the pool before the strike.

After the little ants were tired of swimming, they took a nap on the lawn near the pool.

While the little ants were sleeping, the big ants gathered back at the ant hill. One of them said, "Who is going to take us swimming?"

Another ant said, "Who is going to serve me something to eat?"

Another ant said, "And who is going to clean up my room?"

At last Hawk said, "Stop complaining. We must take care of ourselves."

The other big ants did not say anything for a long time.

More next time.

otter

1. On line 1, write what the big seal swims with.

2. On line 2, write about the seal that swims with fish.

A little mole liked to dig holes. She dug too many holes. At last her mom told her, "Don't dig so many holes near home. Go on the other side of the hill and dig there."

The little mole did that. Later that day, the little mole came back with a big lump of gold. Now all the moles dig on the other side of the hill.

1. What did a little mole like to do?
2. Who told her to dig some where else?
3. What did the little mole find on the other side of the hill?
4. Who digs on the other side of the hill now?

73

1. our
2. proud
3. found
4. round
5. ground
6. house

1. wailing
2. crying
3. howling
4. gathering
5. lasted
6. shouted

1. together
2. chores
3. sacks
4. picked
5. hungry
6. butterfly

1. draw
2. tired
3. tried
4. third
5. net
6. trap

1. work
2. workers
3. cook
4. shook

The Big Strike
Part Five

Hawk told the big ants that they had to take care of themselves. But at first, the big ants just kept on complaining. They said, "We can't do hard work. We are not worker ants. We need somebody to serve us."

By the third day, many big ants were crying and wailing. "I'm hungry," they shouted. "I need food."

By the third day, Hawk was getting tired of listening to the big ants cry and wail. He said, "You can stay here and complain. I'm going to the field and gather seeds."

"Oh good," one of the other ants said. "Bring some seeds back for me."

"No," Hawk said. "I will eat the seeds that I gather."

"But how will the rest of us get seeds?" the ant asked. And Hawk told him.

Hawk took a sack and hiked to the field. Some of the other big ants went with him and picked seeds. After they filled their sacks, they sat down and ate. One of the ants said, "This work is not too hard."

Another big ant said, "You know, I think I like gathering seeds."

Another ant turned to Hawk, smiled, and said, "Burp."

This is not the end.

hay

1. On line 1, write what the thin goat sleeps on.
2. On line 2, write about the goat that sleeps on grass.

One day a farmer saw a big red butterfly and said, "I want that butterfly." The farmer got a net and went after the butterfly. The butterfly landed on top of a bee hive. The farmer took his net and tried to trap the butterfly. The butterfly got away. When the net hit the bee hive, the bees were not happy. They chased the farmer home.

1. Who wanted to get the butterfly?
2. The butterfly was big and ▮▮▮ .
3. What did the butterfly land on?
4. What chased the farmer home?

74

1. f<u>ou</u>rth
2. a<u>round</u>
3. be<u>ing</u>
4. <u>to</u>gether
5. <u>work</u>ing
6. <u>he</u>'ll

1. f<u>ou</u>nd
2. pr<u>ou</u>d
3. felt
4. shy
5. ch<u>o</u>res
6. h<u>or</u>se
7. driv<u>e</u>rs

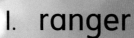

1. ranger
2. blanket
3. problem
4. h<u>ea</u>rd
5. strong
6. f<u>oo</u>t

1. h<u>oo</u>ves
2. shame
3. chin
4. cheek
5. blush
6. speed
7. sleek

The Big Strike
Part Six

By n<u>oo</u>n on the th<u>ir</u>d day of the strike, most of the big ants were working. A lot of them gathered seeds. Three of them drove the ant van. They were not very g<u>oo</u>d drivers, but they agreed, "This is a lot of fun."

Some big ants even started cleaning up the ant hill.

By n<u>oo</u>n on the f<u>ou</u>rth day, all of the big ants were working, and they were pretty pr<u>ou</u>d of themselves.

The next day was the last day of the strike.
That day the big ants got up and did all the chores
that the little ants had done before the strike. One
of the big ants said, "You know, we were pretty
mean to those little ants. We didn't even say
thank you."

Near the end of the last day, Hawk and 20
other big ants went to where the little ants were
playing. The big ants wanted to talk to the little
ants about an end to the strike.

The big ants told the little ants, "We found out that we don't hate hard work."

Homer said, "And we found out that it is not fun to be lazy all the time."

So the ants agreed to end the strike.

Today, big ants are not ordering little ants around. All the ants work together, and when the work is over, all the ants play together.

This is the end.

leaf   stick

1. On line 1, write what the white sheep bit.
2. On line 2, write about the black ant.

A farmer had sweet butter. The farmer said, "Sweet butter makes batter that is never bitter." The farmer started to make batter for rolls.

When the farmer was not looking, the brown fox took the sweet butter and left his bitter butter. The farmer made bitter batter with that butter. Later, the farmer tasted the rolls she baked. She said, "Yuck. Those rolls are bitter."

1. Who was going to bake something?
2. What was she going to bake?
3. Did she start out with sweet or bitter butter?
4. Who took sweet butter and left bitter butter?
5. How did the farmer's rolls taste?

1. h<u>or</u>se
2. h<u>oo</u>ves
3. sh<u>ar</u>p
4. sp<u>ee</u>d
5. sl<u>ee</u>k
6. wast<u>e</u>

1. sky
2. high
3. able
4. table
5. r<u>oo</u>f
6. h<u>oo</u>f

1. know
2. new
3. by
4. buy
5. h<u>ear</u>d
6. cooked

1. <u>l</u>east
2. <u>blank</u>et
3. <u>clean</u>ed
4. <u>wish</u>ed
5. <u>small</u>er
6. <u>snail</u>s

Running

Most animals with legs that live on land don't walk when they want to get away from something or when they chase something. Most of the time, land animals with legs run when they chase something, want to get away, or just want to go faster.

Here are facts about running:

- Animals can run faster than they can walk.
- When animals are running, at some time all parts of them are in the air and no part of them is on land.

If you are running, at some time both of your feet are in the air and not on land.

Here are some pictures of a girl.

Look at the pictures. In any of the pictures is all of the girl in the air and no part of her on land?

The fourth picture shows all of the girl in the air, so the girl is running in these pictures.

An animal is not running if at all times some part of it is on land.

Here are some pictures of a man.

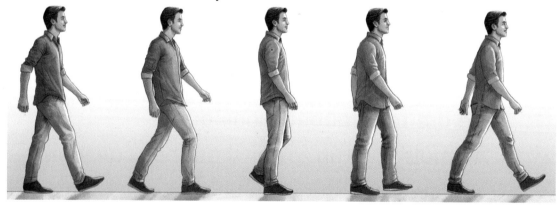

Look at the pictures. In any of the pictures is all of the man in the air and no part of him on land?

At all times, at least one foot is on land, so the man is not running in these pictures.

Here are pictures of a h<u>or</u>se.

At any time are all of its h<u>oo</u>ves in the air? So do these pictures show this h<u>or</u>se running?

Here are other pictures of a h<u>or</u>se. At any time are all of its h<u>oo</u>ves in the air? So, in these pictures, is this h<u>or</u>se running?

bird   leaf

1. On line 1, write what the yellow fly is on.
2. On line 2, write about what is on grass.

One day, a girl's mom told the girl to get out of bed. The girl said to her mom, "I don't want to follow your orders any more. I am going to run away from home."

Her mother said, "You can run away. But if you leave, you won't be able to eat pancakes, eggs, and rolls I've made."

The girl stopped to think and said, "I am hungry, so I will eat."

1. What did the girl not want to do any more?
2. What did the girl say she was going to do?
3. What food did the mom make?
4. Why did the girl stay?

1. knew
2. heard
3. high
4. higher
5. buck
6. wasted

1. sharp
2. pound
3. smallest
4. cheek
5. cleaned
6. horses

1. Agnes
2. ranger
3. blanket
4. sleek
5. hooves

1. he'll
2. shy
3. door
4. chin
5. sees
6. speed

1. cooked
2. behind
3. tables
4. alone
5. smaller
6. Sweetie

A Horse Named Agnes
Part One

Agnes was a very shy h<u>or</u>se who lived on the farm with Gorman and Joan.

Agnes was not a pretty h<u>or</u>se, but she was pretty big. She had h<u>oo</u>ves that were so big that she c<u>ou</u>ld not keep up with the other h<u>or</u>ses when they ran fast. She tried, but her h<u>oo</u>ves were not g<u>oo</u>d for fast running.

Agnes really liked a h<u>o</u>rse named Al, but he didn't care about her. He called her Big F<u>oo</u>t. Every morning, Al went out with a little white h<u>o</u>rse named Bell. They would run and jump and run some more.

Al liked to show off his speed because the ranger was looking for a h<u>or</u>se. Every morning, Al w<u>ou</u>ld ask Agnes, "Do I look sleek today? Is my tail pretty? Do I look too fat?" Agnes w<u>ou</u>ld tell Al that he looked fine. Then he w<u>ou</u>ld go out with Bell and show off. Al kept telling Agnes, "One of these days, the ranger is going to come ar<u>ou</u>nd here. When he sees me, he'll know that I am the h<u>or</u>se for him."

Al kept showing off day after day, but the ranger didn't show up. Then one day, Gorman told a cow that he saw the ranger near the farm. What Gorman really saw was a blanket hanging over a m<u>ai</u>l box. But the cow didn't know that Gorman had seen a blanket, not the ranger.

More to come.

short   dirt   grass

1. On line 1, write about what the long fox ran on.
2. On line 2, write about who ran on grass.

Mark got work as a cook in a f<u>oo</u>d shop. The girl who gave Mark the work told him, "The faster you do things, the more cash we make."

At first Mark cooked f<u>oo</u>d quickly. But when folks who ordered the f<u>oo</u>d tasted it, they said, "Yuck."

Now, Mark doesn't cook quickly. Everybody likes the f<u>oo</u>d they order, and the shop sells lots of f<u>oo</u>d.

1. Mark got a job as a _____ .

2. At first, Mark cooked f<u>oo</u>d _____ .

3. Did folks like Mark's f<u>oo</u>d when he cooked quickly?

4. Do folks like the f<u>oo</u>d Mark makes now?

5. How much f<u>oo</u>d does the shop sell now?

1. sleek
2. sheep
3. higher
4. sharp
5. quiet
6. buck

1. behind
2. alone
3. heard
4. knew
5. less
6. plop

1. farther
2. wished
3. pounding
4. flowing
5. wasted
6. streams

1. house
2. storm
3. blush
4. clapped
5. reading
6. puddle

A Horse Named Agnes
Part Two

Gorman told a cow that the ranger was near the farm. The cow told a horse, and that horse told all the other horses. So almost all the horses went out to show off for the ranger. But before the horses left the barn, they asked Agnes things like, "How do I look? Is my coat smooth and sleek? Does my tail look good?"

Agnes told the other h<u>or</u>ses that they looked fine. Then they quickly ran from the barn up to hig<u>h</u>er hills where they c<u>ou</u>ld be seen for miles.

Poor Agnes w<u>ou</u>ld watch them from the barn. She w<u>ou</u>ld watch them leap, and chase each other, and make sharp turns, and kick, and buck. And she w<u>ou</u>ld think, "Why can't I be quick and sleek like those h<u>or</u>ses?" She w<u>ou</u>ld wish her h<u>oo</u>ves were smaller so that Al would like her more.

The ranger didn't show up that day. And later the horses did a lot of complaining because they wasted a lot of time showing off.

About a week later, the horses heard once more that the ranger was coming to the farm. Two sheep had heard the farmer talking about the ranger's visit. One sheep told a cow. She told a horse, and soon all the horses knew about the visit.

When Al found out that the ranger was coming, he told Agnes, "Follow me around. You won't be able to keep up, but try to stay close."

More next time.

box   green

1. On line 1, write about what the man holds.
2. On line 2, write about who holds a brown leaf.

The <u>qu</u>een of the toads was better at reading than any other toad in the pond. All the other toads came to hear her read. After she was done reading a sh<u>or</u>t story, the toads clapped a little bit. After she was done reading a longer story, the toads clapped more. Did the toads clap even more after she was done reading a very long story? No. Most of the toads were sleeping.

1. Who was the best reader in the pond?

2. What did the other toads do after she was done reading a sh<u>or</u>t story?

3. When she was done reading a longer story, the toads clapped ▢▢▢▢ .

4. Why didn't the toads clap when she was done reading a very long story?

78

1. sticky
2. alone
3. farther
4. pounding
5. flowing
6. turning

1. step
2. felt
3. fell
4. less
5. plop
6. cheek

1. door
2. behind
3. knew
4. second
5. problem
6. awful

1. crows
2. snakes
3. claws
4. sounds
5. tigers
6. spiders

1. mill
2. raw
3. sort
4. taken

Next to you, I look ten times better.

A Horse Named Agnes
Part Three

Al wanted to show off for the ranger, so he told Agnes to stay as close to him as she could.

"I'll try," she said, and she felt very good because Al wanted her around.

But then Al told her why he wanted her near him. "I look wonderful when I'm standing alone," he said. "But when I'm standing next you, I look ten times better. The ranger will pick me in a second."

"Oh," Agnes said, and she felt very sad.

I can't keep up.

On the morning that the ranger was coming to the farm, Al and little Bell were the first ones out of the barn. Al called to Agnes as they left, "Come on, Big Foot, try to keep up." And away they went. But Bell and Al went so fast that Agnes could not stay with them very long. She fell farther and farther behind, and soon she could not see Al and Bell.

So Agnes started walking back to the barn.
And just then, an <u>awful</u> rain st<u>or</u>m began. In less
than ten seconds, the rain was p<u>ou</u>nding down so
hard that most of the h<u>or</u>ses started running back
to the barn.

Before long, streams of water were flowing
down the hills. The fields were turning into lakes.
And the paths were turning into a sea of mud.

The other h<u>or</u>ses were slipping and slid<u>ing</u> in
the mud. But the mud was no problem for Agnes.
Her h<u>oo</u>ves were so big that they almost floated on
the mud. She just walked back to the barn without
slipping once—plop, plop, plop.

This is not the end.

little   clock

1. On line 1, write about what a big man cleaned.
2. On line 2, write about a man who cleaned his shirt.

The queen of the toads was a good hopper. But she could read much better than she could hop. A lot of the other toads were good hoppers, but they could not read very well. The queen told them that she would teach them how to read better. And she did. Now there are a lot of toads that read better than they hop. In fact, some of those toads can read better than the queen.

1. Who said she would teach other toads how to read?

2. At first, some toads could hop better than they could _____ .

3. Now a lot of toads read better than they can _____ .

4. Do any toads read better than the queen?

1. heads
2. yards
3. steps
4. cheers
5. webs
6. beds

1. d**oo**r
2. floor
3. stuck
4. truck
5. took
6. shook

1. so<u>me</u>where
2. an<u>y</u>how
3. <u>m</u>issing
4. <u>m</u>uddy
5. s<u>t</u>icky
6. windo<u>w</u>

1. ti**e**
2. dish
3. str<u>ai</u>n
4. streak
5. nodded
6. blushed

1. material
2. <u>sor</u>ted
3. <u>shi</u>pping
4. work<u>shop</u>s
5. store<u>rooms</u>

A Horse Named Agnes
Part Four

The rain and mud were <u>awful</u>. Almost all of the horses made it back to the barn. But two were missing. Al and Bell were still out in the storm.

At last, the horse standing next to Agnes said, "I'm going to find them."

She ran out of the barn and started up the path. But before she went ten yards, she was stuck in the mud. It took her a long time to make her way back to the barn. She said, "No horse can go in that mud. It's too deep and sticky."

A little while later, one of the horses said,
"Look, look. There's the ranger's truck." It was
hard to see it in the rain, but there it was, near the
farm h<u>ou</u>se. It was stuck in the mud. The d<u>oor</u> was
open, and the ranger was getting out. But after he
took three steps, he was stuck in the mud.

All the horses in the barn agreed that they had to do something to help the ranger. But what could they do? One horse said, "We'll just get stuck if we go out there."

Agnes said, "Well, I think I can go out there without getting stuck."

"No you can't," the other horses said. "That mud is too deep and sticky."

Agnes said, "Well, I think I'll try anyhow."

More next time.

snake

brown

1. On line 1, write about what will go in green grass.

2. On line 2, write about where an ant will go.

Kim and Dan took their bikes to the beach. Kim said, "I won't ride close to the waves because I don't want to get wet."

Dan said, "Ho, ho. I'm going to ride near the waves but I won't get wet."

So they went down to the beach on their bikes. One of them got very wet. The other one said, "Dan got too close to the waves."

1. Who took their bikes to the beach?

2. Who did not want to ride near the waves?

3. Who wanted to ride near the waves?

4. Did Dan think he would get wet?

5. Who got wet?

1. straining
2. dishes
3. blushed
4. heads
5. nodded
6. muddy

1. tied
2. dried
3. long
4. strong
5. hills
6. mills

1. eyes
2. buy
3. shook
4. hip hip hooray
5. ashamed
6. works

1. he'll
2. she's
3. they're
4. I'd
5. she'd

99

A Horse Named Agnes
Part Five

Agnes walked over to the ranger without sinking into the mud one time. The ranger got on her back, and Agnes walked back to the barn, plop, plop, plop. The other horses were shocked. They were saying things like, "Did you see that? I don't know how she does that."

The ranger got off and looked ar<u>ou</u>nd the barn. Then he said, "Where is Al? He's one of the horses I've come to see." The horses shook their heads to tell the ranger that Al was not ar<u>ou</u>nd.

The ranger said, "Do any of you horses know where he is?" Agnes nodded her head up and down.

The ranger grabbed some rope and said, "Well, let's find him." He got on Agnes. She walked from the barn, plop, plop, plop, up the muddy path and up to the higher hills.

They <u>fou</u>nd Al and Bell in a field. They were really stuck in mud. The ranger said, "We'll make a t<u>rai</u>n." He ti<u>e</u>d Bell to Al. Then he ti<u>e</u>d Al to Agnes. Then he got on Agnes and said, "Okay, Agnes, let's tow these two horses back down to the barn."

Three cheers for Agnes.

Getting Al and Bell out of the mud was not easy. Agnes had to strain hard. And at first, she didn't think she would be able to get the train started. But she kept straining. After a while, Al and Bell were able to free themselves. Slowly, the train went down the hills. It took a long time to get back to the barn because Al and Bell kept slipping, sliding, and getting stuck. But at last they made it.

When the train made it back to the barn, the other horses shouted, "Three cheers for Agnes. Hip hip hooray. Hip hip hooray . . ."

Agnes blushed and said, "Well . . . I . . . thank you."

More next time.

rake	girl

1. On line 1, write about who uses a broom.
2. On line 2, write about what a man uses.

Two hundred bees wanted sweet butter. A farmer had sweet butter. So the bees said, "Let's go over to the farm and take that butter." They did not know the farmer baked sweet cakes with his sweet butter. When the bees got to the farm, they did not find any butter. So they took five sweet cakes back to their hive with them.

1. How many bees wanted sweet butter?
2. Who had sweet butter?
3. What did the farmer make with the butter?
4. How many did the bees take?

82

1. ladder
2. raw
3. <u>ou</u>ch
4. weak
5. m<u>ou</u>th
6. number

1. puddles
2. spotted
3. grabbing
4. hated
5. windows
6. towns

1. dart
2. brags
3. gr<u>ou</u>nd
4. snuck
5. dried
6. spend

1. apple
2. growing
3. ashamed
4. buy
5. strong
6. eyes

The ranger should buy Agnes.

A Horse Named Agnes
Part Six

After the ranger left, Al told the other horses, "I am ashamed of myself. I called Agnes Big Foot and made fun of her because she couldn't run fast. But she is the best horse on this farm. I'm going to let the ranger know that she is the horse he should buy."

The other horses nodded and said things like, "Yes, she's something else."

Agnes was so happy that she had big tears in her eyes.

I need a horse that is quick and strong.

A week later, the ranger returned to the farm. The mud was dried up, and the sun was out. The ranger and the farmer walked up to the barn. Al was ready to dart out of the barn and try to let the ranger know that Agnes was the best horse. But he stopped and listened to what the ranger was saying to the farmer.

"Well," the ranger said, "I really need two horses. I need one that is quick and strong. I've seen Al showing off and I want him."

Before Al could do anything, the ranger went on. "I also need a mud horse," he said. "Your horse Agnes is the best mud horse I have ever seen. So I'd like to buy her too."

... And Agnes is the best mud horse there is.

The horses inside the barn cheered. Al was smiling and laughing. Agnes was smiling and crying. And the ranger was happy because he felt that he had found two good horses.

The ranger has had those two horses for three years now, and they never let him down. The ranger brags a lot about them. He'll tell anybody who will listen that he has the two best horses a ranger could have.

The end.

log

1. On line I, write about what is in front of a pig.
2. On line 2, write about what is behind a fox.

Sam the snake wanted to eat a snail. But the snail had another plan. Just as Sam opened his lips to eat him, the snail slipped a hot pepper inside. Sam yelled and darted away. He said, "I don't like to eat snails. They are too hot!"

1. What was Sam?
2. What did Sam try to eat?
3. What did the snail slip inside Sam's lips?
4. Who yelled and darted away?

83

1. pet
2. list
3. ground
4. pole
5. broke
6. driving

1. smelled
2. smiled
3. smallest
4. here
5. there
6. were

1. they're
2. we're
3. they'd
4. he's
5. it's

1. materials
2. shops
3. piles
4. trips
5. loads

Here Pig One. Here Pig Two. . . .

Peppers for Pam's Pigs

Pam had six pigs. Five pigs were big. The pig named Pig Six was very small.

One day Pam didn't have pig food for them. All she had were piles of red hot chili peppers. She had never fed her pigs chili peppers, but she said, "I don't think these hot peppers would bother my pigs. Those pigs eat almost anything."

So Pam loaded some peppers in a pot and some peppers in a pan. She took the pot and the pan of peppers to the pig pen. She set the chili peppers in a pile and called her pigs.

The pigs came and smelled the peppers. But they didn't start eating. Pam said, "I don't have pig food. Why don't you try eating these peppers?"

So the pigs started to eat the peppers. After ten seconds, all of the pigs but one were starting to turn red. Those pigs stopped eating peppers and ran to the drinking tub at the other end of the pen. They drank and drank lots of water out of the tub.

At the same time, they could feel the burn from the chili peppers getting hotter and hotter. The water didn't stop the burn, so those pigs ran here and there, eating dirt and trying to make the hot taste go away. Those pigs ended up being very red.

While the five pigs were drinking water, rolling around on the ground, and eating dirt, the smallest pig kept eating hot peppers. She ate and ate until nothing was left of the pile. Pig Six didn't turn red at all. She was just pink. Pam asked her, "Don't those chili peppers burn you at all?"

Pam's smallest pig smiled and said, "Burp." That was her way of saying thank you.

The end.

bird	horse

1. On line 1, write about what is in front of a car.
2. On line 2, write about what is behind a car.

Bob went out on a sail boat with three pals. A strong wind took the sail boat a long way from shore. Then the wind stopped, so the boat stopped too. Bob told his pals, "I have to be back home by five."

One of his pals said, "How can we get back in time if there is no wind?"

At last, the wind started blowing again, and the pals sailed back to shore. But, when Bob got home, it was after five.

1. How many pals went with Bob?
2. How many pals were on the boat?
3. What kind of boat did Bob and his pals go on?
4. What did the boat do when the wind stopped?
5. Was Bob late when he got home?

84

1. he'd
2. we'd
3. she's
4. it's
5. they've
6. you've

1. <u>shocked</u>
2. <u>smiled</u>
3. <u>creeping</u>
4. <u>landed</u>
5. <u>wider</u>
6. <u>believed</u>

1. sound
2. ground
3. claw
4. raw
5. splash
6. eagle

1. fence
2. thought
3. music
4. word
5. world
6. worst

115

Facts about Vehicles

Many vehicles are machines. Cars, trucks, bikes, ships, trains, planes, and many boats are vehicles that are machines.

Balloons, rafts, hang gliders, and some boats are not machines.

All vehicles take things places. Some vehicles are made to take you and other folks places. Cars, buses, and trains are some of the vehicles that cart folks from place to place.

Other vehicles that take folks and goods places go on water. Can you name some of the vehicles that go on water?

Yes, row boats, sailboats, rafts, and ships are vehicles that go on water.

Can you name the vehicles that go on rails?

Yes, trains must go on rails to get from place to place. Some trains take folks from place to place. Other trains take things and goods.

Can you name vehicles that go in the air?

Yes, planes, gliders, and hot air balloons go in the air.

Can you name vehicles that go on roads?

Yes, cars, vans, trucks, buses, and bikes go on roads.

Some trucks and trail bikes are made to go places that don't have roads. Off road vehicles go slower but take bumps better than road vehicles.

pink

1. On line 1, write about which animal is in a green barn.

2. On line 2, write about which barn a cat is in.

A rat wanted to eat something. She said to herself, "I can get corn from the field and cheese and butter from the farmer's house. I will cook buttery cheese corn on the farmer's stove."

That is what the rat did. When the rat was done cooking, she ate the buttery cheese corn. Yum Yum. When she was done with the corn, she left the cob in the farmer's sink.

The rat was happy. But the farmer didn't know where his butter and cheese went. He also didn't know how a corn cob got in his sink.

1. What did the rat make to eat?
2. What did the rat take from the farmer's house?
3. Where did the rat cook her food?
4. Did the rat like what she ate?
5. What was left in the farmer's sink?

85

1. kind
2. eagle
3. puddle
4. snuck
5. clear
6. slam

1. chirp
2. splash
3. swoop
4. shock
5. ladder
6. floor

1. Bonnie
2. fireman
3. window
4. poles
5. thrown

1. raw
2. law
3. mills
4. shipped
5. sorted
6. materials

Shipping Goods

All vehicles take things places. Most cars and buses and many vans, boats, ships, planes, and trains are made to take folks like you and me places.

Vehicles also ship things places. Vehicles ship raw materials, goods, and food to places all over the world.

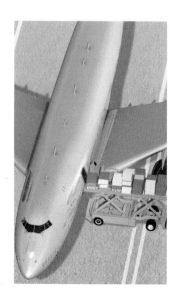

Trucks are almost always used to pick up raw material and take it to workshops or mills. The workshops and mills make that material into goods that are sold. Trucks are almost always used to pick up raw food from farms and take it to mills or workshops that get the food ready to sell.

Most of the time, when mills or workshops have goods and food ready to sell, they use trucks to take the goods and food to a big storeroom. In these big storerooms, the goods and food are sorted for trips in other vehicles. There are many, many of these storerooms in every big town.

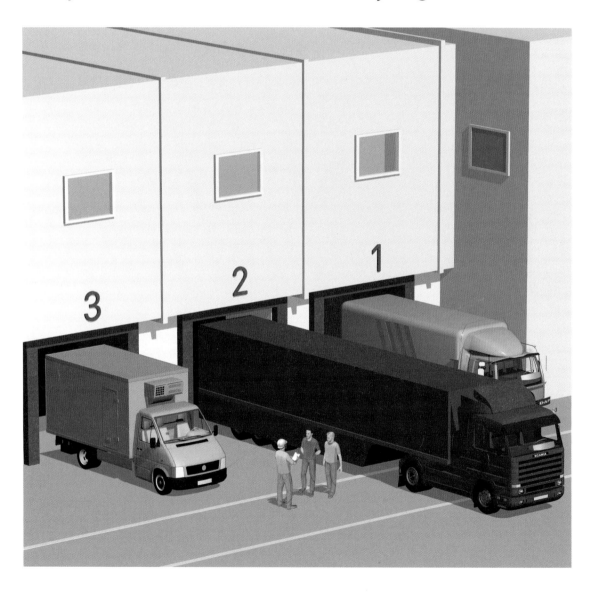

Goods and food are sent from the storeroom to other storerooms, to stores, or to houses or shops. If the goods or food are going somewhere not very far from the storeroom, they are shipped by truck or van. If the storeroom is very far away, the food or goods may be loaded into trains, ships, or planes for a trip to a storeroom that is closer to where those things are going.

After the trip, the goods and food are taken off the planes, trains, or ships and loaded into the closer storeroom. In the closer storeroom, the goods or food are sorted again for their last trip. Workers at the closer storeroom load the goods and food into vans or trucks that will take the things to the stores, the homes, and the shops where they are going.

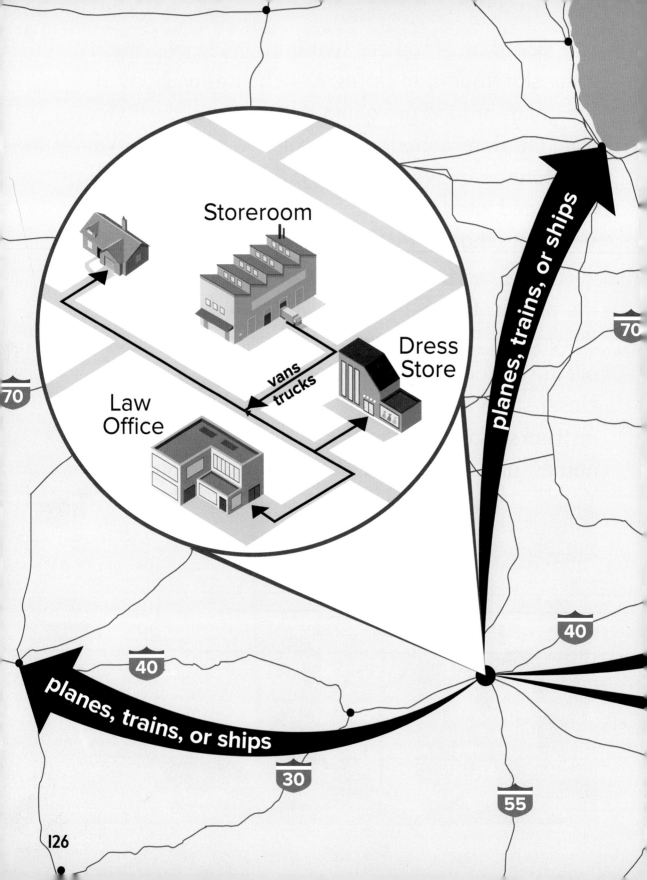

Storeroom

Dress
Store

vans
trucks

Law
Office

planes, trains, or ships

planes, trains, or ships

70

70

40

40

30

55

126

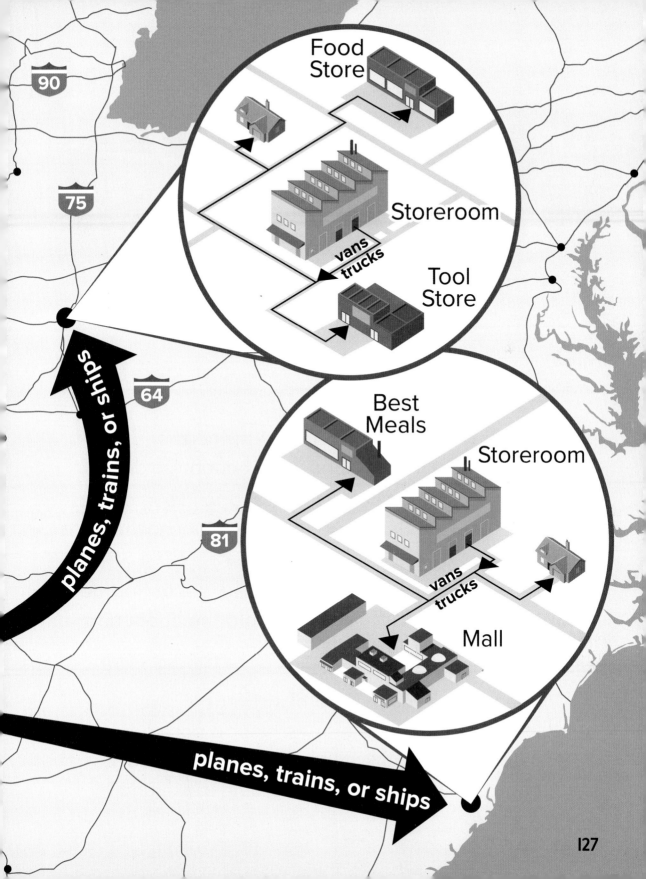

Food
Store

Storeroom

vans
trucks

Tool
Store

Best
Meals

Storeroom

vans
trucks

Mall

planes, trains, or ships

planes, trains, or ships

brown

1. On line 1, write about which barn a goat is in.

2. On line 2, write about a cow.

A baboon was tired of staying at the zoo. "I want to live in a forest near a pond," the baboon said.

A goose told the baboon, "I used to live in a forest near a pond." And the goose told the baboon where the forest and pond were.

The baboon asked, "But how will I get out of the zoo and to the forest?" The goose told the baboon to order a hot air balloon and float there.

1. Where was a baboon tired of staying?
2. Who wanted to live in a forest near a pond?
3. Who said, "I used to live in a forest near a pond"?
4. The goose told the baboon to order ▬▬▬ and float there.

86

1. own
2. yum yum
3. pet
4. spotted
5. slammed

1. across
2. careful
3. helpless
4. watered
5. whenever

1. Bonnie
2. Sweetie
3. fence
4. thought
5. kinds

1. watching
2. splashing
3. chirping
4. swooping
5. flapping
6. wondering

1. children
2. dizzy
3. jumping
4. fixing

Sweetie and the Bird Bath
Part One

Bonnie really liked birds. One day, she saw some birds cleaning themselves by splashing in a puddle. She said to herself, "Those birds shouldn't have to take a bath in a puddle. They should have a bird bath."

She kept thinking about the bird bath. She liked that plan. She said to herself, "I'll buy a big bird bath. It will be so big that any bird who needs to get clean can come to my yard and jump in the bird bath."

Yum, yum.

So Bonnie went to the pet store and got the biggest bird bath the store sold. She set up that bird bath in her yard. And soon, birds started to gather in the bird bath. These birds called to their pals, and before long, the bird bath was filled with all kinds of birds—yellow birds, red birds, brown birds, and spotted birds.

Bonnie watched all these birds, but she wasn't the only one watching them. A big yellow cat lived next door. That cat's name was Sweetie, but that cat wasn't sweet at all. When Sweetie saw all those birds, he said to himself, "Yum, yum."

As Sweetie watched and watched, he made up a plan. He said to himself, "I will sneak over to that bird bath. Then I will jump up before the birds know I am ar<u>ou</u>nd. I'll grab two or three of them before they can get out of the water. Yum, yum."

More to come.

<table>
<tr><td>rope</td><td>yellow</td></tr>
</table>

rope	yellow

1. On line 1, write about which cat played with a ball.
2. On line 2, write about a black cat.

Don was a cook who was neat. He worked at a place called the Fry Shop. Don didn't leave batter or sticky food on the pots and pans he used. Don didn't leave dirty cups in the sink. Don cleaned up everything in the sink after he was done cooking.

1. Where did Don cook?
2. Was Don a neat cook?
3. Did Don leave batter on things?
4. What did Don clean up after he was done cooking?

87

1. b**ea**k
2. str**ea**k
3. s**ou**nds
4. m**ou**th
5. cl**aws**
6. **ou**ch

1. w**ea**k
2. bunch
3. p**a**rk
4. snuck
5. list
6. spends

1. fence
2. car**e**ful
3. th**ough**t
4. eagle
5. o**w**n

1. **paint**ed
2. **flapp**ing
3. **swoop**ed
4. **chirp**ing
5. **slamm**ed

1. **be**come
2. **on**to
3. com**plain**ed
4. **different**

Sweetie and the Bird Bath
Part Two

Sweetie had a plan. And he was ready to start doing what he planned.

He snuck into Bonnie's yard. He went into some long grass near the fence. Very slowly, he snuck closer and closer to the bird bath. He was careful not to make a sound. At last, he was almost under the bird bath. He was now ready to leap up and grab two or three birds.

flap

chirp

chirp

flap

But just as he was ready to spring up, he heard a lot of flapping sounds and chirping. Sweetie stopped and waited for the birds to quiet down.

Sweetie couldn't see the top of the bird bath. So he didn't see why all the birds were chirping and flapping their wings. Sweetie didn't know that an eagle had swooped down to take a bath. When the other birds saw the eagle swooping down with its big claws and sharp beak, they took off. Those birds left the bird bath as fast as their little wings could take them.

Things were quiet now. Sweetie thought that the little birds were still in the bird bath. So he got ready to spring up and grab two or three little birds. He didn't know that there were no little birds in that bird bath. There was only one bird—an eagle that was about three times as big as Sweetie.

Sweetie took a big leap. He landed on one side of the bird bath. He landed with his claws out, grabbing at the first thing he could reach. Things happened so fast that Sweetie really didn't see the eagle clearly. He grabbed the eagle, and in less than a second, the eagle grabbed him with its big claws. The eagle picked Sweetie up and slammed him down in the bird bath. Splash. Ouch.

More next time.

black	grass

1. On line 1, write about what a brown cat sat on.

2. On line 2, write about which cat sat on a rug.

Henry was an ant. He was very scared of spiders. He was scared of their long legs and the way they jumped. Henry didn't like the sticky webs they made. Most of all he was scared of getting stuck in a web.

Henry thought, "There are no webs in my ant hill. I will stay home." So Henry cleaned and served other ants at the ant hill. Other ants left the ant hill to gather seeds and other food.

1. What was Henry?
2. Who didn't like spiders?
3. What was Henry most scared of?
4. Where did Henry stay?
5. What did other ants do when they left the ant hill?

138

88

1. <u>w</u>ondering
2. <u>reach</u>ing
3. help<u>less</u>
4. when<u>ever</u>
5. <u>across</u>

1. children
2. number
3. merry
4. whisper
5. right
6. fight

1. streak
2. m<u>ou</u>th
3. spends
4. weak
5. park

1. music
2. woman
3. fence
4. ra<u>ce</u>
5. i<u>ce</u>
6. <u>thou</u>ght

1. rain<u>ed</u>
2. chop
3. share
4. stare
5. sudden

Sweetie and the Bird Bath
Part Three

Sweetie hated water, and he was all wet.

Sweetie's ears went back, and he shot out of that bird bath so fast that he looked like a yellow streak. He darted out of Bonnie's yard and back into his yard.

Then he hid under his h<u>ou</u>se. He had his m<u>ou</u>th open and his eyes were very wide.

"What happened?" he said to himself. "One second I was reaching out for a little bird, and the next second I was getting slammed into the water."

Sweetie wasn't looking at the bird bath. He never saw the eagle. And while Sweetie was hiding under his house, the eagle left. As soon as the eagle left, all the little birds returned to the bird bath.

At last, Sweetie came out from under his house and looked at the birds around the bird bath. He saw the same little birds he saw before. Sweetie looked at those birds for a long time. Then he said to himself, "From here, those birds look pretty small and weak. But when you get close to them, they are really big and strong. I don't think I'll ever go near that bird bath again."

So now Bonnie is happy because her bird bath always has a lot of pretty birds in it. The birds are also happy because they can meet all their pals and have a bath whenever they want. The only one who is not happy is Sweetie. Sweetie spends a lot of time looking at the birds in Bonnie's yard, but he never goes over there. Sweetie also spends a lot of time wondering how those birds can look so small and weak, but be so big and strong.

The end.

green

1. On line 1, write about which room is dirty.
2. On line 2, write about the red room.

Scott had a baby cat that went up a tree. Scott went up the tree to get the baby cat down. He went very high in the tree and got stuck.

He called for help, and after a while, a cop came. The cop went up the tree to get Scott down. The cop went so high he got stuck too. At last a fireman came with a long ladder. Scott, his baby cat, and the cop came down the ladder. When Scott was on the ground, he told the fireman, "Thank you."

1. Where did Scott's kitten go?

2. Did Scott try to get the kitten down?

3. Who got stuck trying to get Scott down?

4. Who got them all down?

1. Rolla
2. merry-go-round
3. music
4. children
5. racing
6. number

1. forward
2. unhappy
3. quicker
4. onto
5. thrown
6. raining

1. dog
2. wood
3. work
4. worst
5. world
6. woman

1. hardly
2. closely
3. dizzy
4. jumpy

1. chopped
2. wagged
3. sharing
4. trading
5. plate

Rolla
Part One

There once was a wonderful merry-go-round in a park. Everybody liked that merry-go-round. The music would play, and the horses on the merry-go-round would go up and down with children on them. The music was good. The horses were pretty. So the mothers were happy, and the children were happy.

146

Almost all the horses were happy. But one horse was not happy at all. That horse was named Rolla. She was not happy because she had a big 8 painted on her side. There were only 8 horses in the merry-go-round, and she was horse 8. So she thought she was in last place.

As Rolla went up and down, she kept thinking, "Why should I be horse 8? Why can't I be horse 5 or horse 3?" She was as big as the other horses. She went just as fast as they did. So why couldn't she have a better number?

The more she thought about it, the more she thought she would like to be number 1. That would be the best number a horse could have. But how could she get a better number?

For days she thought about it. Then she said to herself, "The only way I can get a better number is to go faster. If I pass the horse in front of me, I'll be horse number 7, and that horse will be horse 8. If I pass all the other horses, I'll be number 1."

More next time.

cat   socks

1. On line 1, write about what is under a snake.

2. On line 2, write about what is behind a snake.

Ted was lazy. He didn't work around the house. Ted didn't do anything. One day, Ted's mother told Ted, "If you don't do work around our house, you'll have to go live somewhere else."

Ted asked, "What work do I have to do to stay here?"

His mother gave him a list. So Ted watered the lawn, washed the dishes, and cleaned the floor. Now every day, Ted does the work on a list from his mother.

1. If Ted didn't work around his house, he would have to live _____ .

2. Ted's mother gave him a _____ .

3. Write two of the things Ted did.

4. Does Ted do the work on the list every day?

91

1. dizzy
2. jumpy
3. closely
4. hardly
5. quietly

1. poles
2. swing
3. bunch
4. fix<u>ed</u>
5. quick<u>er</u>
6. cloth<u>e</u>s

1. wǫrd
2. wǫrst
3. wǫrld
4. worked
5. wondered

1. ri<u>gh</u>t
2. diff<u>e</u>rent
3. whisp<u>e</u>red
4. racin<u>g</u>
5. forward
6. nodding

1. mess
2. cut
3. pat
4. fir
5. flash
6. string

Rolla
Part Two

Rolla was horse number 8, but she wanted to become horse number 1. She knew that there were 8 horses on the merry-go-round. So she'd have to pass all the other horses. She didn't know that her plan couldn't work.

On the next day, she tried to pass the other horses. And she tried very hard. She started to go faster. She went up and down quicker, and she went forward faster. But when Rolla went faster, all the other horses had to speed up too. Even the music went faster.

That fast merry-go-round did not make the mothers or the children happy. The horses were going up and down so quickly that the children could hardly hang on to them.

The merry-go-round was turning around too fast for the mothers to stand next to their children. The mothers had to hang on to the poles to keep from being thrown off. But they went so fast that their feet went flying in the air. When the merry-go-round stopped, everybody was dizzy.

One mother got off the merry-go-round and said, "This is the worst merry-go-round in the world. Even the music is jumpy and bad."

The horses on the merry-go-round didn't like it any better than the mothers did. They were getting sore and tired from jumping up and down and racing like the wind. They kept yelling at Rolla, "Slow down. This is not fun." But all day, she kept trying to pass the horse in front of her. But she couldn't do it.

And at the end of the day, she was as sore and tired as the other horses.

More next time.

small   **mole**

1. On line 1, write about who dug a big hole.

2. On line 2, write about an ant.

Jim told all his pals, "I like to go on long hikes. I can hike up any trail there is."

One day, Jim walked up and down three steep trails. Then he came to a very big hill. He hiked up that hill for a long time. He did not reach the top of that hill. When he came back, he complained.

Jim said, "I don't like to go on long hikes very much after all."

1. At first, who liked to go on long hikes?
2. How many steep trails did he walk up and down?
3. Did he reach the top of the big hill?
4. Does he like to take long hikes now?

92

1. howl
2. nut
3. shak<u>e</u>
4. fool<u>ed</u>
5. dinn<u>er</u>
6. diff<u>er</u>ent

1. ice
2. ri<u>ght</u>
3. knows
4. eye
5. w<u>oo</u>d
6. ro<u>w</u>ing

1. <u>peach</u>
2. <u>string</u>
3. <u>follows</u>
4. <u>whispering</u>
5. <u>suddenly</u>
6. <u>bunch</u>

1. every
2. summers
3. sometimes
4. painting

1. put
2. pull
3. warm
4. dog
5. lose
6. friend

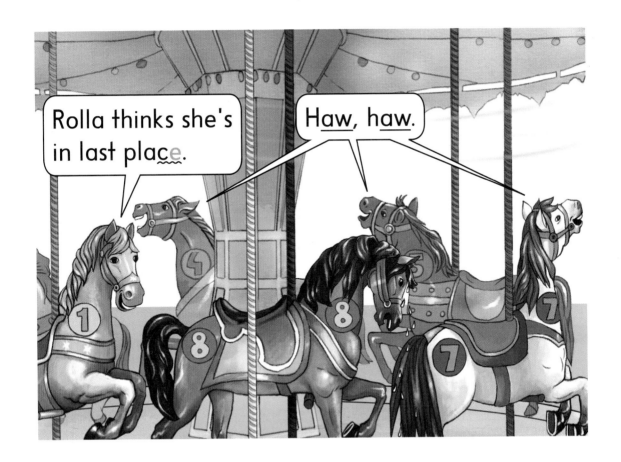

Rolla
Part Three

Rolla was tired and very sad. "I'm tired of being number 8," she told the other horses. She had a tear in her eye. "But I can't seem to pass the horse in front of me to get out of last place."

"Is that your problem?" horse number 1 asked. "Do you think your number shows that you are in last place?"

All the horses gave Rolla a big horse laugh.

Horse number 3 said, "Numbers don't mean anything. Every horse follows the other horses and every horse is in front of the other horses."

"Yes," horse number 5 said. "If you look behind you, you'll see you're right in front of horse number I. So you are really in front of all the other horses."

But Rolla didn't believe this. After they talked and talked, she still said, "But I'm number 8, so I must be the last horse on this merry-go-round." She had another big tear in her eye.

The other horses whispered to each other and nodded their heads up and down. They had a plan. After some more whispering and nodding, horse number 2 said, "Rolla, if you had a different number, would you stop trying to go fast?"

"Yes, yes," she said.

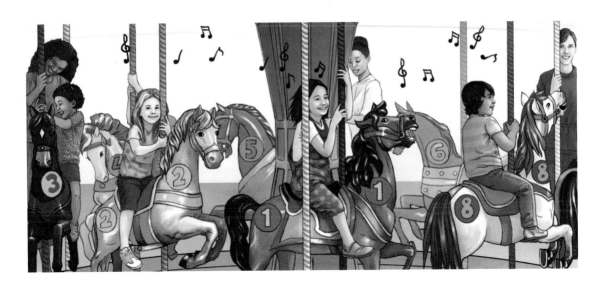

When it was dark, the horses worked hard painting and fixing things up to make everybody happy.

So if you go to Rolla's merry-go-round today, you won't hear any mothers complaining about the music or about horses racing around. You won't see children who are scared. You won't see mothers hanging on to poles as hard as they can. You'll see a happy bunch of horses going around at a good speed. You'll hear music that is pretty and not jumpy. You'll see children laughing and mothers smiling. You'll also see that the horses are smiling. And if you look very closely, you'll see that one horse has a bigger smile than the other horses. That horse is number I, and her name is Rolla.

The end.

dog

1. On line 1, write about what is behind a bus.
2. On line 2, write about a goat.

Today it rained. The storm started before the sun came up, and it rained until after dark. It was raining when I woke up. It was still raining when I went to bed. The sun didn't shine all day.

Long after it was dark, the rain stopped and the storm went away. They say that it will not rain for more than a week.

1. All day long it ▮▮▮▮▮.
2. When did it start raining?
3. Did the sun shine at all?
4. How long do they say it will not rain?

1. st<u>oo</u>d
2. wood
3. chopp<u>ed</u>
4. dropp<u>ed</u>
5. star<u>e</u>
6. share

1. evening
2. i<u>c</u>e
3. ra<u>c</u>e
4. shak<u>e</u>
5. nuts
6. wag

1. <u>suddenly</u>
2. per<u>son</u>
3. con<u>test</u>
4. <u>out</u>side
5. <u>sweep</u>ing
6. <u>loud</u>er
7. <u>hun</u>gry

1. put
2. loses
3. friends
4. cloth<u>e</u>s
5. dog
6. cook

Waldo and the Hungry Dog
Part One

Waldo was an old man who was very poor. He lived by himself in a small house that was near a forest. There was a lake that was about a mile from Waldo's house.

In the summer, Waldo liked to walk to the lake and fish. He liked the hot sun. Summers were good for Waldo, because there was a lot of food around. There were apples and nuts growing on trees. He could also pick and eat beans, leaves, and seeds from other plants. So Waldo was never hungry in the summer time.

But winter was no fun for W<u>a</u>ldo. He would always run low on food before spring came. He would even run out of wood for his fire. There was lots of wood in the forest, but that wood was under three feet of snow. There were nuts on the ground, but the nuts were under three feet of snow.

There were lots of fish in the lake, but there was snow on the lake, and below the snow was ice. To get fish, Waldo had to clear the snow away and then chop a hole in the ice.

Waldo would drop his fishing line into the water and wait for a fish. Sometimes, he would have to wait a long time before he got one. Sometimes, the wind would howl, and the cold air would make Waldo shake.

More next time.

water   pail   woman

1. On line 1, write about who filled a hole with dirt.
2. On line 2, write about what a girl filled.

A crow saw a big nut on the ground. The crow said, "I think I'll eat that nut." So the crow grabbed the nut and started to fly away with it.

Just then the nut said, "Set me down."

The crow dropped the nut and said, "I never saw a talking nut before."

A bug came out of the nut and said, "I am not a talking nut. I am a talking bug. This nut shell is my home."

1. Who saw the nut on the ground?

2. What did the crow want to do with the nut?

3. What was inside the nut?

4. The bug told the crow that the nut shell was his ▓▓▓▓ .

94

1. warm
2. oven
3. woman
4. put
5. dog

1. shut
2. sweep
3. c<u>ou</u>nt
4. lev<u>er</u>
5. memb<u>er</u>
6. stamp

1. <u>dress</u>ed
2. <u>suddenly</u>
3. <u>pat</u>ted
4. <u>clear</u>ed
5. <u>evening</u>
6. out<u>side</u>

1. plate
2. stared
3. flash
4. chopped
5. clothes
6. dream

1. cut
2. bed
3. pie
4. share
5. wag
6. l<u>ou</u>d

Waldo and the Hungry Dog
Part Two

One year was very bad for Waldo. He got sick in the fall and did not pick very many apples and nuts. Winter started suddenly, with a cold wind and lots of snow. Soon Waldo was low on wood for his fire and had only two apples. He said to himself, "I'll have to get some fish from the lake."

So Waldo put on lots of clothes and hiked to the lake.

He cleared the snow and chopped a hole in the ice.

He fished most of the day. But he only got
three small fish. He said to himself, "These fish
won't make a very good meal." Then he hiked
back to his house. On the way, he saw a big dog
near the forest. The dog looked very thin. The dog
followed Waldo, walking slowly far behind him in
the deep snow.

When Waldo got home, he went into his house, leaving the dog outside. That evening, Waldo cooked the three fish. He set out one of his apples, and he was just sitting down to eat.

Suddenly, a howling sound came from outside. At first, Waldo believed it was the wind. The howling sound came again. So Waldo got up and opened the do<u>or</u>. There was the big dog that Waldo had seen before. The dog stared at Waldo with a sad look, and then the dog's tail started to wag.

Waldo said, "You look cold and hungry. Come in. It is not cold in here."

The dog came inside.

"You poor dog," Waldo said. "I wish I had food to share with you. But all I have is three small fish.

The dog wagged her tail again.

More to come.

dog   table

1. On line I, write about what a cat is on.
2. On line 2, write about what animal is on a floor.

A dog and a cat played with a ball of string. They were in the front yard of their house. The cat stood on one end of the string. The dog ran with the ball of string. The dog ran around and around the yard. The ball of string got smaller and smaller as the dog ran around. Soon there was no ball of string, but there was a mess in the front yard.

1. Who stood on one end of the string?
2. Who ran with the ball of string?
3. Did the ball of string get bigger or smaller?
4. What did the front yard look like?

95

1. lie
2. pry
3. lever
4. clever
5. butter
6. cutter

1. quietly
2. quickly
3. patted
4. sharing
5. dressed

1. person
2. alone
3. dinner
4. soaking
5. hunting
6. wagging

1. friend
2. dogs
3. warm
4. put
5. woman

1. plate
2. fir
3. shut
4. dream
5. flash
6. speaks

Waldo and the Hungry Dog
Part Three

Waldo let a big, thin dog into his house.

Before Waldo started to eat, he took an old coat and put it on the floor. "This will keep you warm," he said to the dog.

Waldo patted the dog. Then he sat down at the table to eat. He looked at the dog. The dog did not howl or cry. The dog just stared at him, and Waldo could see that the dog was very hungry.

Waldo looked at the three fish. Then he looked at the dog again. He said to himself, "I can not eat without sharing what I have." Then he said, "Come over here and have one of my fish."

The dog sat next to Waldo, and Waldo gave a fish to the dog. The dog ate it quickly. Waldo started to eat a fish. The dog sat quietly and watched him eat. Waldo ate the fish slowly. Then he looked at the last fish and said to the dog, "You need this more than I do." And he gave his last fish to the dog.

All at once, the dog turned into a pretty woman dressed in white. She said, "You are a very good man, Waldo. You were hungry, but you gave me most of what you had. So, from this day on, you will never be hungry or cold again."

Then there was a flash, and Waldo was all alone in his house. He was sitting on his bed. He said, "It must have been a dream."

This is not the end.

pie

1. On line 1, write about what the woman baked.
2. On line 2, write about who baked a cake.

A rat had some bitter butter. He saw Gorman and said to himself, "I'll bet I can talk Gorman into trading me something for this bad butter."

The rat asked Gorman, "What will you trade me for this sweet, sweet butter."

Gorman was not fooled. Gorman said, "If you let me have that butter, I will let you take a row boat out on the lake."

The rat said, "I like row boats."

So the rat went rowing in the boat. But it wasn't long before he was all wet.

After the rat got out of the lake, he said, "I hate toads who sink boats."

1. Did the rat want to trade or sell the butter?

2. Was the butter sweet or bitter?

3. What did Gorman let the rat do on the lake for the butter?

4. Who sank the boat while the rat was rowing?

96

1. thought
2. bought
3. brought
4. right
5. night

1. ice
2. cent
3. lace

1. contest
2. person
3. dinner
4. remember

1. yeah   4. friend
2. love   5. along
3. heard

1. smiling
2. fires
3. dreamed
4. shouting
5. rooms
6. mixed

1. fur
2. smoke
3. crust
4. spent
5. crisp
6. stamp

Waldo and the Hungry Dog
Part Four

Waldo was sitting on his bed. He thought he had dreamed about the dog and the woman. He got up and said, "I will eat my dinner now."

He looked where he kept his apples, but he did not see two old apples. He saw a pile of big, sweet apples. "What is this?" he said. "Who put these apples here?"

Waldo picked up an apple and went to where his three small fish were. But he did not see three small fish. He saw three very big fish. "I can not believe what I see," he said.

Just then, he heard a sound at the door. He opened the door. In the snow was the dog, but now the dog was not thin and hungry. The dog seemed to be smiling as she looked at him.

"Come in, my friend," he said. "Come in. We will have a fine dinner. And you may stay for as long as you wish."

The dog stayed with the old man and was his friend from that day on. Waldo was never hungry again. His house was never cold. And if somebody who was alone and hungry came to Waldo's house, there was always food and a warm room for the person to stay. Waldo would tell the person, "We are glad we have so much that we can share it with you."

The dog would wag her tail to show that she agreed.

This is the end.

snake   boat   green

1. On line 1, write about which boat the goat is in.

2. On line 2, write about the snake.

A woman had a sick oak tree in her front yard. She called someone to cut down the tree. She told the tree cutter, "I live at 1234 Elm Street. Cut down the big oak tree in my front yard."

The tree cutter did not show up. The woman was going to call that person after she went on a walk. She walked along Oak Street and suddenly she said, "I know what happened. The tree cutter went to 1234 Oak Street and cut down an elm tree. Oh dear."

1. What was the name of the street the woman lived on?
2. What was the street number?
3. Did she want the tree cutter to cut down an oak tree or an elm tree?
4. What kind of tree did the tree cutter cut down?

97

1. egg
2. fur
3. pies
4. spent
5. sweep
6. contest

1. goldfish
2. cooking
3. counting
4. stamping
5. speaking

1. bought
2. brought
3. night
4. right
5. tight

1. lose
2. pull
3. looks
4. yeah
5. word
6. worm

1. once
2. race
3. cent
4. fence

The Cooking Contest
Part One

When the bragging rats did not agree, they made things bad for the other rats. Those rats had to listen to the bragging rats go on and on. One of the worst times the other rats had was when the bragging rats started bragging about how good they were at cooking. Their bragging about cooking came after they spent a day yelling about how good they looked. That fight started when the rat with yellow teeth said that he looked better than any other rat in the world. The rat with the long tail said, "How can you say such lies? You look like a goldfish with fur and big yellow teeth. I am the one with the good looks."

The other rat said, "Oh yeah? Your tail looks like a long thin snake, and your nose looks like a lump of mud."

For the rest of that day, those rats yelled and shouted about how good they looked. The other rats were glad when night came and the bragging rats stopped yelling.

But the next morning, they started it all over again. This time, the rat with the long tail said, "Did you know that I am the best cook in the world?"

"You never cook anything," the rat with the yellow teeth said.

The rat with the long tail said, "Well, everybody knows why I don't cook much. My cooking is so good that I would eat too much if I cooked, and I would get too fat."

The rat with the yellow teeth said, "You lie like a rug. You don't even know how to heat water on a stove."

Those rats went at it all morning—yelling, shouting, stamping their feet, and telling big lies.

More to come.

dog

1. On line 1, write about what is behind a fox.
2. On line 2, write about what is in front of a ram.

There were a lot of cats that lived in a room in a farmer's house. That room had lots of cat fur on the floor. A goat had to keep the floor clean. He would sweep the floor with a broom. At the end of each day, the farmer gave the goat something to eat. One day, the goat worked all day sweeping fur. But at the end of the day, the farmer did not give the goat any food so the goat ate the broom.

1. What did the farmer have a lot of?
2. The room they lived in had lots of ▩▩▩ on the floor.
3. Who would sweep the floor?
4. When the farmer did not give the goat food, the goat ate ▩▩▩ .

98

1. places
2. laces
3. rice
4. once
5. race

1. <u>wouldn't</u>
2. <u>fanning</u>
3. <u>baking</u>
4. <u>peaches</u>
5. <u>block</u>
6. <u>across</u>

1. oven
2. remember
3. crust
4. lose
5. word
6. <u>bar</u>

1. eggs
2. pies
3. c<u>ou</u>nt
4. speak
5. skates
6. smoke

The Cooking Contest
Part Two

The bragging rats had been yelling all morning long. They were telling lies about how well they could cook. The rat with the long tail was saying, "I'm not only the best cook in the world, I'm the fastest cook in the world. My eggs are cooked before you can c<u>ou</u>nt to three."

Some of the other rats in the pack went to the wise old rat and said, "Isn't there something we can do to make those bragging rats shut up?"

"Yes, there is," the wise old rat said. "We will have a cooking contest. That should keep them quiet."

The wise old rat walked over to where the bragging rats were. The rat with the yellow teeth was saying, "I can fix a pie so fast that it's done before you can count to one."

The other rat said, "My pies are bigger and better than any pie you can fix. And I can bake five pies before you can bake one pie."

The wise old rat said, "Stop bragging and listen to me. We will have a contest to see who makes the best pie. But you must not say a word while you make your pie. If a rat speaks, that rat will lose the contest. And the rat that loses must never brag about cooking or anything else for a year."

The wise old rat asked the bragging rats, "Do you agree?"

"Yes, yes," they said.

The rat with the yellow teeth said, "I will be so quiet that nobody will know I am making the best pie in the world."

"Oh yeah?" the other rat said. "I will be so quiet that nobody will even know that I am in a baking contest."

The bragging rats spent the rest of the day bragging about how quiet they would be while baking their pies.

More to come.

1. On line 1, write about what a small dog wore.

2. On line 2, write about which dog wore a green shirt.

Peg and her cat lived in a place that was too small. She said, "Let's go find a place that is bigger." She saw one home she liked, but she did not have the cash to live there. She saw another place that was nice, but that place would not let her keep a cat. She looked and looked for weeks. At last, she thought of a great plan. She told her cat, "I will put two rooms onto our home, and that will make it much bigger." That's what she did.

1. Who did Peg live with?
2. Why didn't she like her home?
3. Did Peg go to another place to live?
4. What did she put onto her home?

99

1. soft
2. pulls
3. puts
4. loved

1. face
2. coal
3. brick
4. crawl
5. crust
6. smoke

1. baking
2. fanning
3. oven
4. remember

1. freeze
2. skate
3. crack
4. shelf
5. blade
6. crisp

1. houses
2. peaches
3. mittens
4. plates
5. stairs
6. robbers

The Cooking Contest
Part Three

The next morning, the wise old rat met the rat pack in a field. He had two old ovens that burned wood. He told the bragging rats that they had to get all the things they needed to make their pies. The other rats would bring wood for the fires. Then each bragging rat would make a fire in his oven and bake a pie. The other rats would taste the pies and pick a winner.

The wise old rat said, "And remember, the rat that loses the contest must never brag for one year."

After the bragging rats left to get the things they needed to make their pies, the wise old rat led the other rats to a big pile of fire wood. That wood had been soaking in the pond. It looked dry on the outside, but it would not burn well because it was wet on the inside. The wise old rat said, "This wood will take a long time to burn well. That will make the bragging rats stay quiet all day."

Soon the bragging rats were ready to start baking. The rat with the yellow teeth had all the things he needed to make the pie crust. He also had a bag of apples. The rat with the long tail had peaches.

Those rats stared at each other, but they didn't say a word. They loaded the wet wood into their ovens and tried to start the fires, but the wood wouldn't burn. The rats tried fanning the fires and blowing on them. The only thing this fanning and blowing did was make a lot of smoke. Smoke rolled out of the ovens, but the wood did not really burn. All day long the bragging rats worked on their fires. And they were both quiet. That made the other rats very happy.

More next time.

boot   hanger

1. On line 1, write about what the shirt is on.

2. On line 2, write about what the boot is on.

Two turtles wanted a swimming pool. One turtle said, "A swimming pool would take a lot of cash. We don't have that cash."

The other turtle said, "We could make a swimming pool."

So they dug a big hole. Then the turtles filled the hole with lots of water. Did they have fun swimming in their pool? No. The water in the hole mixed with the dirt to make a lot of mud. The turtles did not like their pool of mud. But their six pig friends said, "This is the best pool ever."

1. Who wanted a swimming pool?
2. Did they have the cash they needed?
3. After they dug a big hole, what did they fill it with?
4. Who liked their pool?

101

1. night
2. fight
3. soft
4. skate
5. blade
6. coal

1. own
2. love
3. loser
4. put
5. pull
6. push

1. crisp
2. freeze
3. crack
4. shelf
5. crawl
6. brick

1. mittens
2. lever
3. laces
4. counted
5. barking

203

The Cooking Contest
Part Four

That night, the wise old rat soaked the wood again. But in the morning, the rat with the long tail came to the field with his own wood. He smiled at the rat with yellow teeth, but he didn't say a word. He put his dry wood on top of the wet wood that was in the oven.

In no time, his oven had a big fire in it.

That fire was so hot that it dried out the wet wood, and that wood started to burn. Soon the oven was so hot that it began to turn red on the outside.

The rat with yellow teeth saw what the other rat did, so he ran off to the forest to get some dry wood. He came back with two times as much wood as the other rat had. He smiled and put the wood on top of the wet wood in the oven. Soon his oven was red hot on the outside, too.

The other rats watched. One rat whispered to the wise old rat, "If they put their pies in such hot ovens, they will burn to a crisp."

Those ovens were so hot that the rats could not stand near them without getting burned. But the rat with yellow teeth got an oar. He put his pie on the end of the oar and put it in the oven. The oven was so hot that it burned the oar. The rat with the long tail also got an oar and put his pie in the oven.

Then the rats waited and waited before they tried to get their pies out of the ovens. When they got their pies out of the ovens, the other rats started to laugh and howl. Those pies looked like round black bricks. One of the other rats said, "I don't want to taste those pies to see which one is best."

The only two rats that didn't laugh were the bragging rats. The one with yellow teeth said, "This contest was not fair. This is not a good oven."

The other rat said, "Yeah, look at how this bad oven turned my wonderful pie black as coal."

The wise old rat said, "You both talked, so you both lose. That means you both have to stop bragging for a year."

The bragging rats didn't like that, but they kept their word and didn't brag for one year.

The end.

1. On line l, write about what the hat is over.
2. On line 2, write about what is under a cake.

One day, a hunter was out hunting for lions. He saw two tigers, an ape, a snake, and six birds. But he didn't see any lions.

At the end of the day, the hunter still had not seen any lions. He said, "I am going home because there are no lions around here."

As he was driving away, a hundred lions came out of the hills. One of them said, "That hunter is not very good at finding lions."

1. What was the hunter hunting for?

2. He saw tigers, birds, a snake, and ▨▨▨▨▨ .

3. Where did the hunter go at the end of the day?

4. What was the hunter doing when the lions came out?

102

1. thief
2. pry
3. kid
4. blade
5. ties
6. girls

1. <u>owner</u>
2. <u>loudest</u>
3. <u>barks</u>
4. <u>rocked</u>
5. <u>opening</u>
6. <u>freezing</u>

1. bought
2. brought
3. pull
4. soft
5. off
6. love

1. <u>skating</u>
2. <u>crawling</u>
3. <u>mittens</u>
4. <u>hands</u>
5. <u>cracking</u>
6. <u>shelf</u>

Be Careful, Ann

We each have a blade, and we each have laces. We come out in the winter, but we don't come out as much as we would like. We are kept in a dark place that has lots of coats and mittens and other things girls put on in the winter. Do you know what we are?

Yes, we are ice skates, and we love to go ice skating.

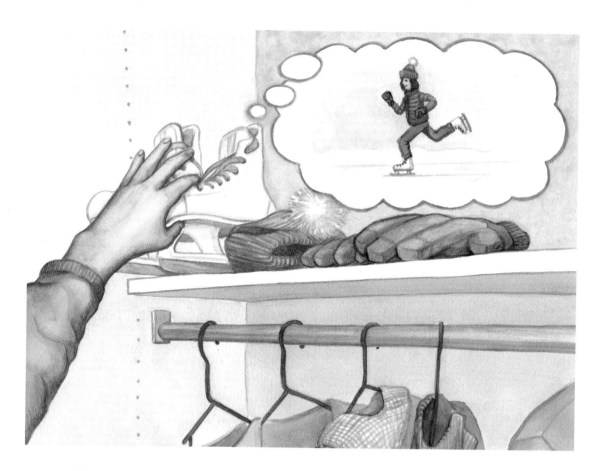

We sit on a shelf and wait a long time for very cold days. We want all the water in the pond to freeze and become ice. We want to slide over that ice. Yes, yes, yes. Skating is what we look forward to all year.

Now the door to the room is opening. A hand is reaching to grab us. It's Ann's hand. She pulls us off the shelf and takes us with her. This is it. Ann will put us on, and we will go skating. Yes, yes, we really want to go. We remember how good it feels to have our laces tied around Ann's foot inside.

When we reach the pond, Ann puts one foot inside each of us. Now she pulls on the laces and ties them. Now we are on the ice. Wow, we are going fast. Now we are leaving the hard ice and going on ice that is thin and soft. Suddenly, the ice is cracking. We are dropping into the freezing water. Brrr.

Now we are crawling out. Brrr. Ann is taking us off. She is not having fun. She will sit with us to dry in front of a fire when we get home.

Next time, Ann will skate where it is safe.

The end.

road

1. On line 1, write about what the rock is on.
2. On line 2, write about what animal is near the toad.

Ed was a little kid who loved to count things. He counted eggs. He counted trees. He counted dogs, cats, and bees. When he went on a walk, he counted the houses he walked by. He counted the cars on the street. He even counted stairs and chairs.

One day his mother said, "Oh dear. I had ten fine plates, but I can see only seven of them here. Three plates are not here."

Ed said, "Two of your plates are in a box, and one of your plates is on a shelf in the front room."

Ed's mom went to the box and found two plates. She went to the shelf in the front room and found the other plate. She said, "Ed, you are so smart."

1. What did Ed love to do?

2. What was his mother looking for?

3. Did Ed know where they were?

4. Where were two of the plates?

5. What room was the third plate in?

103

1. bars
2. wire
3. thief
4. wakes
5. bent
6. chomps

1. today
2. farther
3. lifted
4. picture
5. becomes
6. inches

1. levers
2. roosters
3. using
4. prying
5. spending
6. pounds

1. wood
2. strong
3. heavy
4. pulled
5. words
6. works
7. head

Levers

You can use thin strong bars to lift heavy things. When a bar is used to lift things or pry things, it becomes a tool called a lev<u>er</u>.

A rock that is too heavy for big men to lift with their hands can be lifted by children with a lev<u>er</u>. One end of the bar goes under the rock.

There is a green part that shows how far up the rock will be lifted. Someone at the other end of the lev<u>er</u> pulls down on it. The red part shows how far down that end needs to be pulled. The number on the rock shows how heavy it is. The number near the end of the lev<u>er</u> shows how hard that end needs to be pulled down to lift the rock.

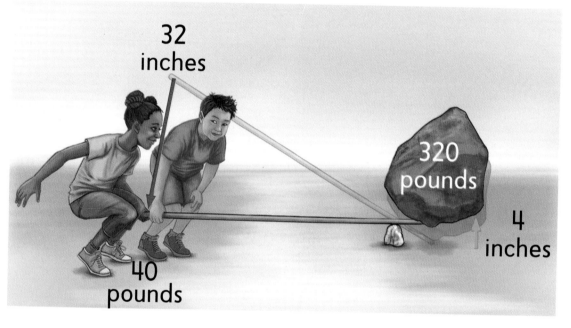

- How heavy is the rock?
- How hard does someone need to pull down to lift the rock?
- How far does the green part show the rock will be lifted?
- How far does the red part show that someone will pull on the lev<u>er</u>?

Here's a rule about this kind of lev<u>er</u>. You lift more p<u>ou</u>nds than you pull with, but you pull a lot farther than you lift.

Here's a picture of a lev<u>er</u> used to pry nails out of wood.

There is a claw on the end of this lev<u>er</u>. To lift a nail, you slide the claw under the head of the nail. Then you pull on the other end to pry the nail out of the wood.

1. On line 1, write about who writes with a yellow pen.

2. On line 2, write about what a woman writes with.

104

1. ranger
2. stranger
3. large
4. charge
5. ridge
6. bridge

1. Doris
2. Art
3. bed
4. thief

1. block
2. wake
3. barks
4. bent
5. stack
6. peace

1. spending
2. teaching
3. owner
4. loudest
5. robbing

1. angry
2. meow
3. verse
4. along
5. brought

221

Art the Barking Cat
Part One

Doris lived in a place where she could not have a dog. But she wanted a dog because there was a thief who was robbing a lot of houses around her house.

That thief broke into the house next door to the one Doris lived in. That thief also broke into a house across the street.

Doris didn't know what to do. She thought and thought about it. At last, she went to a pet store and told the owner, "I need a watch dog, but we can't have dogs where I live. What can I do?"

The pet store owner said, "Well, you could buy Art."

"Who is Art?" Doris asked.

The pet store owner said, "Art is a watch cat."

"A watch cat?" Doris said. "That is silly. There is no such thing as a watch cat."

"Yes, there is," the owner said. "His name is Art."

Doris did not believe the owner. She said, "I have no time for bad jokes." She was getting ready to leave the pet shop when the owner brought out a big brown cat with big yellow eyes. The owner said, "This is Art, the watch cat."

Doris said, "He doesn't look like he could scare a robber very much."

The owner said, "Watch this." He put his hands over his ears and said, "Speak, Art."

Art let out the loudest bark that Doris had ever heard. That bark was so loud that it rocked her and made her put her hands over her ears.

"What . . . what was that?" she said.

"That was Art. He barks, and he's a very good watch cat."

Doris said, "That cat is just what I need." She bought Art and took him to her home.

More to come.

cake

1. On line 1, write about what is on top of a can.
2. On line 2, write about what a cat is on top of.

Jim was a mean pig. He would run around the farm every day and bite sheep, horses, and cows. The farmer said, "If you do not stop biting, I will keep you in a pen all by yourself."

Jim said, "I like to bite." He kept biting, so the farmer put him in a pen.

Jim was sad. At last, Clarabelle came up to Jim. She said, "To get out of this pen, you have to stop biting us. If you must bite, bite other things, like cans or pans or sticks or bricks."

Jim listened to Clarabelle and did what she said. After a while, the farmer let Jim out of the pen. He has a lot of friends on the farm now, and whenever he feels like biting, he chomps down on a big stick or an old can.

1. Who liked to bite?

2. What kind of animal was Jim?

3. Where did the farmer put Jim?

4. Did the farmer let Jim out of the pen?

5. What kinds of things does Jim bite now?

105

1. block
2. beds
3. wakes
4. wire
5. please
6. bent

1. haystack
2. windows
3. tiptoe
4. loudly
5. picnic
6. maybe

1. finally
2. rooster
3. happening
4. along
5. sting
6. crowd

1. age
2. stage
3. large
4. barge
5. light
6. bright

Art the Barking Cat
Part Two

Doris brought Art home and fixed up a place for him to eat and sleep. On the first night she had him, a dog walked into the yard. Art let out a bark that sent leaves blowing from the trees. That bark was so loud that folks on the next block almost fell out of their beds. The poor dog in the yard got so scared that he ran like a shot, howling all the way home.

The next night, a cat came into the yard, and Art let out a bark that shook the windows. It also made that cat shake for the rest of the night.

A lot of folks complained about the barking. They told Doris, "You can't have dogs in your place." Doris tried to tell them that she didn't have a dog, but they did not believe her. They said, "If we hear any more barking, we are calling the cops."

The next night, they called the cops. A robber and two of his pals robbed the house next to Art's house. Then they snuck into Art's yard. When they were right next to the house, Art stuck his head out of the window and let out the loudest bark you have ever heard.

That bark sent the robbers flying. Two of them landed in a small tree. Another one landed on the fence. Ouch.

Before the robbers could collect the things they had robbed and get away, the cops came. The cops were looking for a barking dog, but they f<u>ou</u>nd robbers. After the cops took the robbers to jail, they asked Doris about her dog. They didn't believe her story until she told Art to speak. Now they believe her.

Doris still has Art, and once in a while, Art barks at night. He wakes up the folks all along the street, but they don't care, because no robbers come to that street any more.

The end.

boat road

1. On line 1, write about what a bus went on.
2. On line 2, write about what went on a lake.

Don bragged about how good he was at reading and playing baseball.

One day, Bonnie was walking home when she saw Don. He was sitting on the side walk with his head in his hands. Bonnie asked, "Why are you sad?"

Don said, "I tell folks I am good at reading and playing baseball. But I can't read well. I can't play baseball well. I don't have any friends because I brag too much."

Bonnie said, "I will teach you how to read and play baseball well. And I will be your friend."

And Bonnie did those things. Soon Don was spending so much time doing things well that he didn't have time to brag.

Now Don has a lot of friends because he doesn't brag. His best friend is his first friend, Bonnie.

1. What did Don brag about?
2. Who told Don she would be his friend?
3. What did she teach Don to do well?
4. How many friends does Don have now?
5 Does Don have time to brag now?

106

1. edge
2. hedge
3. charge
4. large
5. own
6. known

1. wire
2. tired
3. tried
4. cried

1. rooster
2. haystack
3. tiptoe
4. unless

1. won
2. son
3. find
4. mind
5. lash
6. crash

1. cloud
2. bent
3. task
4. held

1. cock-a-doodle-do
2. Clarabelle
3. angry
4. peace
5. animal
6. finally

Clarabelle and the Birds
Part One

Clarabelle was a cow who lived on the farm with Gorman. One day, Clarabelle was looking at the birds who were sitting on a wire. That wire went from the barn to a large, tall pole. Clarabelle said, "I would love to sit on that wire with those birds."

Some of the other cows listened to Clarabelle talking to herself. One cow said, "Don't do it, Clarabelle. Remember what happened when you tried to swim like a duck in the duck pond?"

"Yes," another cow said. "When you jumped in the pond, all the water jumped out of the pond."

Another cow said, "And what about the time you tried to crow like a rooster? That made me laugh. You sat on the fence with the roosters. They were saying cock-a-doodle-do. But you were saying cock-a-doodle-moo." The cows started to laugh very loudly.

"That's not funny," Clarabelle said. "And if I want to sit on that wire with those birds, you can't stop me."

So Clarabelle went into the barn and up the stairs to the window. The wire was outside that window. While she was getting ready to walk out on the wire, all the farm animals gathered around.

Gorman said, "Tell me what is happening so I don't miss anything."

At last, Clarabelle tiptoed out on the wire, but she was so big that the wire bent down lower and lower with each step. Clarabelle walked out on the wire until it was down near the top of the haystack.

This is not the end.

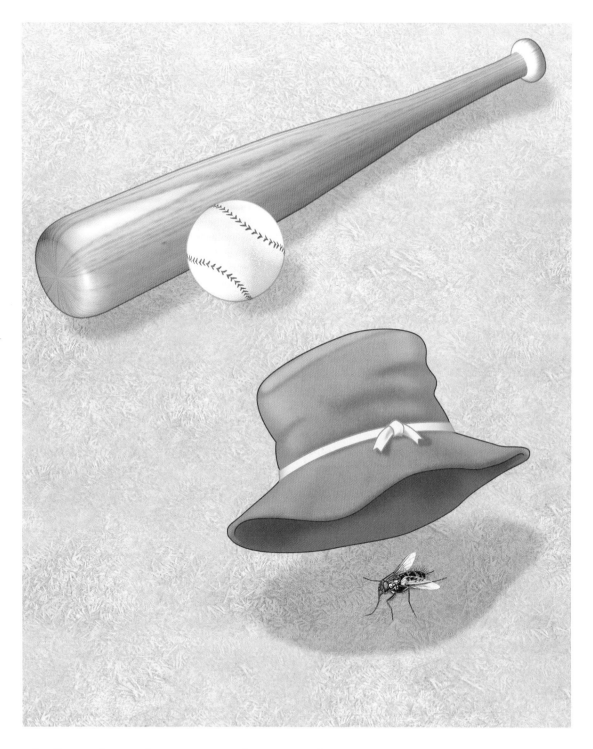

1. One line l, write about what the ball is next to.
2. One line 2, write about what the fly is under.

Bob was always late. When he went on a hike with his pals, he came home late. When he took a trip to the beach, he came home late. When he went sailing, he came home late.

One day, he was talking with a pal named Fred. Bob said, "Fred, I'm always late."

Fred said, "I think I know what you need."

"What's that?" Bob asked.

Fred said, "A watch."

Bob said, "I would like a watch, but I can't tell time."

Fred smiled and said, "Well, you are in luck. I am good at teaching how to tell time."

And so Fred showed Bob how to tell time.

1. Who was always late?

2. Did Bob have a watch?

3. Did Bob know how to tell time?

4. Who said that he would teach Bob to tell time?

5. Did Fred do that?

107

1. choose
2. verse
3. please
4. strange
5. peace

1. rhyme
2. boy
3. great
4. won
5. finally

1. awake
2. die
3. cried
4. flies
5. ropes

1. angry
2. clouds
3. light
4. bright
5. fright
6. sight

1. picnic
2. bus
3. swell
4. task
5. owned
6. puff

Clarabelle and the Birds
Part Two

The birds were angry. They shouted at Clarabelle. One of them said, "Get off this wire. It's for birds, not big cows."

"Yes," another bird said. "We don't like sitting this close to the ground. So get off our wire."

The cows and goats and pigs and sheep were laughing and rolling around on the ground.

Clarabelle was not happy. She said to herself, "Being on this wire with the birds is not as much fun as I thought it would be."

Clarabelle thought about going back into the window, but then she said, "It would be very hard to walk all the way up that wire."

Then Clarabelle looked down and said, "I am so close to the ground that I could jump off and land on the haystack."

As she thought about her plan, the birds kept yelling at her. "Get off our wire so we can sit in pea̰c̰ḛ," they cried.

"All right, I'll leave you alone," she said to the birds. And she jumped off.

When she jumped off, the wire shot up into the air. It shot up so fast that it sent the birds way up into the clouds, leaving feathers all over the place.

The farm animals were laughing so hard that they could not stand up. The birds that had been on the wire didn't laugh. And one cow kept saying, "It's not funny."

But the rest of the farm animals thought it was very, very funny.

This is the end.

car   star

1. On line 1, write about what is next to the moon.

2. On line 2, write about what is in front of a rat.

A mole was lonely. She went looking for a friend. The mole bumped into a duck and asked, "Will you be my pal?"

The duck said, "You can't swim, so I won't be your pal."

Later, the mole bumped into a hawk and asked the hawk to be her friend. The hawk told the mole that they couldn't be friends because the mole couldn't fly.

The next day, the mole bumped into another mole. They were both looking for friends. Those moles became good friends.

1. What did the mole go looking for?
2. The duck wouldn't be the mole's friend because she couldn't ▓▓▓▓▓▓ .
3. The hawk wouldn't be the mole's friend because she couldn't ▓▓▓▓▓▓ .
4. The mole became friends with another ▓▓▓▓▓▓ .

108

1. swell
2. horns
3. ch**oo**se
4. vot**e**
5. task
6. ra**c**ed

1. sta**ge**
2. picnic
3. stran**ge**
4. won
5. boy
6. move

1. Donna
2. school
3. enter
4. parent
5. teacher
6. rhyme

1. please
2. v**er**se
3. gr**ea**t
4. meeting
5. fri**ght**
6. si**ght**

245

Donna
Part One

Donna was a girl who looked like a lot of other girls. But she did one thing that was strange. She talked in verse. When she stood near the bus stop, she would say things like this, "I hate to wait and get there late."

If somebody asked her what time it was, she would say something like this, "I'll let you know then. It's almost ten."

If you met her on the street and asked her how she was doing, she would say something like this, "I hope you can tell that I'm doing swell."

When I'm done with this cake, I'll swim in the . . .

Sometimes her mom and dad would get angry with her for always talking in v<u>er</u>se. Once they were going to a picnic. Her mom said, "Please don't speak in v<u>er</u>se, Donna. Just talk the way the rest of us do."

Donna said, "You gave me a very hard task, but I'll try to do what you ask."

"Oh dear," her mom said, and shook her head.

Donna said, "Maybe I should not even say one word. I won't be bad if I can't be heard."

But at the picnic, she spok<u>e</u>, and she spok<u>e</u> in v<u>er</u>se. Some folks thought she was funny. Some of the others thought she was very stran<u>ge</u>.

A little boy asked her, "How can you talk like that all the time?"

She said, "It's something I don't think about. I open my mouth, and the words come out."

The boy said, "But can you make yourself talk the right way?"

She said, "I don't think that I'm able to. I speak the way I do."

The boy shook his head and took a bite out of his hot dog. He said, "You could go on TV. You're funny."

More to come.

can

1. On line 1, write about what an ant is inside.

2. On line 2, write about what a cow is in front of.

There was a bug who had a rug. That bug took the rug with her every place she went. She took the rug to school. She took the rug to the store. She took the rug with her when she went to play. She even took the rug to bed with her. One day her mom told her, "That rug is getting dirty. I will take it and clean it for you."

But the bug would not let go of the rug. The bug said, "I will wash the rug myself." So the bug took the rug into the lake with her and washed it.

1. What did the bug have?
2. Name two places she took the rug.
3. Who told her that the rug was dirty?
4. Where did the bug wash the rug?

109

1. lash
2. crash
3. bright
4. sight
5. find
6. mind

1. alive
2. unless
3. stings
4. held
5. choose
6. blast

1. rhymed
2. schools
3. parents
4. teacher
5. spots
6. voted

1. motor
2. nice
3. stage
4. die
5. fright
6. meeting

Donna
Part Two

Donna talked in verse. Donna told herself to talk the way everybody else did. And she tried. But the only time she didn't speak in verse was when she didn't know a word that rhymed.

Once she said, "My name is Donna. And I am . . . " She stopped because she didn't know a word that rhymed with Donna.

Then one day, her teacher told her that all of the classes were going to put on a contest to see who could make up the best verse. In a little over three weeks, the children in the contest would read their verse at a large meeting.

Donna made up verse after verse, but she could only read one verse. She didn't know which one to choose. She asked her teacher. "Miss Brown," she said, "please help me choose. And pick the verse that will not lose."

When her teacher was done reading all of Donna's verses, she told Donna, "I really like three of them. I could read those three to the class and see what the children think."

So Miss Brown told the children, "I will read these verses to you, and you will vote for the one you like the best." Ten children liked Donna's verse about the sea. Ten children liked her verse about winter.

Donna said, "We have a tie, so which will it be? The one about winter or the one about the sea?"

The teacher said, "Let's ask another class." And they did. That class voted for the verse about the sea.

The time went by quickly, and soon the day of the contest had come. All the children who were in the contest had to stand up on a stage in front of lots and lots of parents and children and read their verse.

Most of the children in the contest were pretty scared. So was Donna. Just before she was ready to go on stage, she said to her mom, "I don't think my verse is right. And I think I'll die of fright."

"No, no," her mom said. "Just stand up there and tell everybody about the sea. You'll do fine.

More to come.

1. bow
2. bow
3. lead
4. lead
5. does
6. does

Ben   Sandy

1. On line 1, write about who had green boots.

2. On line 2, write about the boots Sandy had.

Two sisters were standing on the beach near the water. The little sister said, "I hope we don't see sharks. I'm scared of sharks."

The big sister said, "Ha, ha. I am not scared of sharks. All the sharks know me. I swim with sharks. The sharks are my pals."

Just then, a big shark came over the waves.

The little sister ran away. But the big sister ran away faster. She was scared.

Later, the little sister said, "Why did you run from that shark? Was that a shark you didn't know?" She knew that her big sister told a lie. Her big sister did not have any shark pals.

1. Who was standing on the beach?
2. Who said she was scared of sharks?
3. Who said that she wasn't scared of sharks?
4. The big sister said, "The sharks are my ⬜⬜⬜."
5. Write how many shark pals the big sister really had.

PHOTO CREDITS

L067 34 (tl)quintanilla/iStock/Getty Images, (tc)lzflzf/123RF, (tr)Tony Vingerhoets/Alamy Stock Photo, (cl)Brenda Carson/Shutterstock, (cr)Christopher Kimmel/Aurora Photos/Getty Images, (bl)Glow Images/Getty Images, (br) sainthorant Daniel/Shutterstock; **L067 35** (tl)ftwitty/E+/Getty Images, (tr)Walter Miller/Alamy Stock Photo, (cl)Westend61/Getty Images, (cr)Arno Images/Cultura/Getty Images, (bl)ArtMarie/E+/Getty Images, (br)ilfede/123RF; **L067 36** (t) Valery Kalantay/Shutterstock, (b)baona/iStock/Getty Images; **L067 37** (tl) Dcjan Milinkovic/Shutterstock, (tc)Christian Weibell/iStock/Getty Images, (tr)svetlanasf/123RF, (bl)Hasan cemal Sargin/Getty Images, (br)steamroller_blues/Shutterstock; **L075 071** Chase Swift/Corbis/Getty Images; **L076 081** Carlo A/Moment/Getty Images; **L084 116** (1)Steve Boyko/Shutterstock, (2)lzflzf/123RF, (3)Tony Vingerhoets/Alamy Stock Photo, (4)Brenda Carson/Shutterstock, (5)Christopher Kimmel/Aurora Photos/Getty Images, (6)Glow Images/Getty Images, (7) sainthorant daniel/Shutterstock; **L084 117** (1)Cathy Yeulet/123RF, (2)Walter Miller/Alamy Stock Photo, (3)Westend61/Getty Images, (4)Arno Images/Cultura/Getty Images, (5)ArtMarie/E+/Getty Images, (6)ilfede/123RF; **L084 118** (1)Shutterstock/Valery Kalantay, (2)William Barton/Getty Images, (3)svetlanasf/123RF, (4)Hasan cemal Sargin/Getty Images, (5)steamroller_blues/Shutterstock; **L085 125** volkan sengor/E+/Getty Images; **L088 144** Intherayoflight/Shutterstock; **L089 150** Inti St Clair/Blend Images LLC; **L101 209** TomazKunst/iStock/Getty Images; **L103 219** Roland IJdema/Shutterstock; **L107 244** grimplet/123RF; **L107 250** Mytho/iStock/Getty Images; **L107 257** Mint Images/Mint Images RF/Getty Images.